Nalule's TRAVELS *and* ADVENTURES

WRITING FOR SURVIVORS IN AFRICA

The Autobiography of
Dr Helen Liebling

First published in Australia by Aurora House

This edition published in Australia by Aurora House 2023
www.aurorahouse.com.au
Copyright © 2023

Typesetting and e-book design: Cognition Technology |
www.cognition-technology.in
Cover Designer: Donika Mishineva | www.artofdonika.com

The right of Graham Blewitt to be identified as Author of the Work has been
asserted in accordance with the Copyright, Designs and Patents Act 1988.

ISBN number: 978-1-922913-56-2 (Paperback)

Distributed by: Ingram Content: www.ingramcontent.com
Australia: Phone: +613 9765 4800 |
Email: lsiaustralia@ingramcontent.com
Milton Keynes UK: Phone: +44 (0)845 121 4567 |
Email: enquiries@ingramcontent.com
La Vergne, TN USA: Phone: +1 800 509 4156 |
Email: inquiry@lightningsource.com

Contents

Glossary of Terms   vi

Acknowledgements   viii

Preface   ix

1. Dancing into the World   1

2. Fun and Family Crises   17

3. Adventures and Fun in Wales   27

4. How Far Can You Travel with £70 and a Tent?   35

5. Tropical Snorkelling, Personal Dilemmas and
    Navigating High Security   43

6. A Scottish Journey into African Music   51

7. Amadinda and Embaire – Wild Xylophones of Uganda   59

8. Adventures in the South African Sea and Nepalese
    Mountains   67

9. Supporting Survivors and Musical Adventures in Uganda   73

10. Bernard – A Chicken on the Bus   79

11. Women Survivors and the Power of Music   83

12. Cuban Rum, Dodging Rubber Bullets, and a Wedding   91

13. The Power of Writing in the Fight for 'Justice'   101

14. Saving Babies and Navigating Security Threats   109

15. Wild Swimming through COVID to an African Future   119

References   129

Glossary of Terms

Amadinda	Wooden xylophone from the central region of Uganda
APRO	African Psycare Research Organisation
BBC	British Broadcasting Corporation
Boda Boda	Motorcycle used for transport in Eastern Uganda
BREXIT	Withdrawal of the United Kingdom from the European Union
Caixa	Brazilian snare drum
CLAMP	Community wellbeing and mental health project among refugees in Uganda
DFID	Department for International Development
DRC	Democratic Republic of Congo
ECT	Electroconvulsive therapy
ESRC	Economic and Social Research Council
Embaire	Ugandan wooden xylophone from Busoga, Eastern Uganda
Endingidi	Ugandan tube fiddle
Endongo	Thumb piano from Busoga, Eastern Uganda
Gyile	Ghanaian wooden xylophone
HIV	Human Immunodeficiency Virus
IRA	Irish Republican Army
Isis-WICCE	Isis Women's International Cross-Cultural Exchange
KIWEPI	Kitgum Women's Peace Initiative
MP	Member of Parliament
Nsassi	Ugandan shaker
PhD	Doctor of Philosophy
SGBV	Sexual and Gender-Based Violence
Timba	Brazilian hand drum
TIA	Transient ischemic attack
UHT	Ultra Heat Treatment
UK	United Kingdom

UN	United Nations
UNHCR	UN Refugee Agency
USA	United States of America
VIVA VOCE	Oral examination for a doctoral degree
VVF	Vesicovaginal Fistula
WANEP	West Africa Network for Peace Building
WIPNET	Women in Peace Building Network
WIPC	Women's International Peace Centre (formerly Isis-WICCE)
WOMAD	World of Music, Arts and Dance
YMCA	Young Men's Christian Association

Acknowledgements

I give sincere thanks to my writing group, 'Ink Plotters', for their helpful comments on some chapters. I am particularly appreciative of Chris, who has spent time reading this book and offering beneficial improvements. She kept me laughing at times when I needed it.

I am grateful to friends who were there for much needed tea, cake, and encouragement. I thank the Sambassadors of Groove Samba Band; playing and performing with the group really kept me positive during isolated times. I am also glad that I started wild swimming and salsa dancing, as these activities kept me energised during COVID and its aftermath, and brought hours of enjoyment and fun, as well as new friends.

I give my appreciation to colleagues in Africa, the United Kingdom and elsewhere who have supported my journey, writing, and research. This includes those involved in establishing the service for urban refugees in Kampala, Uganda.

For those who have given their permission, I have cited their real names and images. For those I could not contact, I have used pseudonyms to protect their anonymity. This autobiography is written from the author's perspective and reflects my subjective thoughts and experiences.

Preface

The road in Goma was black, and rugged, and difficult to walk on. Benoit, my Congolese colleague and friend, informed me that this was due to the fact the volcano had erupted near the town some years back, and the lava had covered the streets.

The streets were heaving with people wearing stunning, bright colours and bustling with energy, whilst navigating the spiky road resulting from the volcanic ash. In the distance, I observed the cause of the road problems and the volcano towering above the town. What was it that led me to this lively region of Africa?

All will be revealed.

Nalule's Travels and Adventures: Writing for Survivors in Africa

The Autobiography of Dr Helen Liebling

Introduction

This is a fascinating autobiography of a feminist, activist and researcher who acted against atrocities and abuses of conflict survivors of Sexual and Gender-Based Violence (SGBV) and torture to aim to improve survivors' rights to health, health care, and justice internationally.

Helen's early life of disruption and family separation led to a passion for advocating for the rights of those who were mistreated. The first musical trip to Uganda shaped Helen's life and she developed a love for Africa, her people, and the traditional music. You will be enchanted by various traditional musical stories. Helen's travels took her to some of the most beautiful places in the world, including African deserts and mountains and waterfalls in Latin America and Africa.

Helen's professional life straddled two different worlds; that of academia and health care services in the United Kingdom, as well as conflict survivors of gender-based violence and torture in Africa, including refugee survivors. Helen's PhD in Women and Gender led to a greater political and humane passion for women's and survivors' rights, particularly in the African continent. As well as being awarded the Phil Strong prize for her PhD, she was presented with a research prize in Johannesburg in 2009 for an outstanding research presentation on her collaborative work with The Women's International Peace Centre in Uganda together with Liberian African women's organisations on Liberian women conflict survivors.

The human rights abuses Helen listened to in conflict-affected countries sharpened her resolve to continue this work after her PhD and she travelled to different African countries, including the Eastern Democratic Republic of Congo, to highlight the experiences of survivors of human rights abuses. Helen vividly recalls how these experiences influenced her decision to work with refugee survivors of SGBV and torture from South Sudan who were living in refugee settlements in Northern Uganda. Helen also assisted to establish a refugee well-being service in the UK and is implementing her integrated model of service provision for urban refugees in Kampala.

The final chapter details Helen's current life, including the impact of COVID, discovering a love for wild swimming and her hopes for the future. Fascinating, emotional, and uplifting, *Nalule's Travels and Adventures: Writing for Survivors in Africa*, is a captivating narrative of hardship, resilience, and triumph against the odds, told with passion and clarity by a woman who never gave up!

One

Dancing into the World

I came bouncing into this world in the early hours of Wednesday, 22 November 1961, in a hospital on Loveday Street in Birmingham, following my mum's rock-and-roll dancing the evening before. *This must explain my love of music and dancing*, I thought to myself when my mother related this story to me. I also remember my dad telling me that when I was a baby (see photo next page), my mother – who was still a medical student at the time (my parents met at medical school) – used to take me in to the medical school and ask the women in the canteen to look after me while she attended lectures. The women were extremely happy to do so, and I always thought that was one of the reasons I am so sociable and friendly with people.

As a child, I can recall my dad saying, 'I remember well when you were two years old'.

'What happened?' I responded, intrigued by his statement. My dad was not usually very talkative, so when he spoke, I knew it was something important.

'Oh, Len', my mum laughed, knowing what he was going to say.

'Me and your mum took you for dinner at a very posh restaurant in the centre of London', continued Dad. 'We were there for a medical reunion. You had a steak which the waiter cut up into small pieces for you, and you finished it off completely'.

'That is strange, since I am now a vegetarian', I remarked whilst my mum continued laughing. I suspect she'd had a little too much to drink.

'Then afterwards', continued my dad, 'you ate two whole caramel custards'.

'But Dad, I hate caramel custards', I said as I listened to my dad recount this story. I had become a vegetarian when I went to university at nineteen, and I still dislike caramel custards.

1

Me as a baby

My dad recounted that he came from a Jewish family. He told me that when he married my mum, his parents – who had wished him to marry a Jewish woman – wore black for two years and would not speak to us. I remember thinking about how my mum was pregnant when she married my dad. I expect if his parents had known, they would have made the whole situation even more challenging.

One of my earliest childhood memories was of visiting my dad's parents in Nottingham. The house was huge and had several floors, which seemed to me to almost reach the sky. I found it interesting to explore but remember thinking that my grandpa was a quirky character. He was a tall, imposing figure who I felt a bit scared of, but he could amuse me when I had hiccups by getting me to drink water out of a glass backwards. I was impressed by this, as it used to work, stopping the hiccups to my great relief.

Another early memory was the excitement of going to my Jewish cousin Kevan's Bar Mitzvah, to celebrate as he 'became a man' in Jewish faith at thirteen years of age. My mother insisted on getting myself and my sister Ruth matching hot pants, which I quite liked. However, she then presented me with a bright pink dress, which I hated with a vengeance. The Bar Mitzvah weekend event was extremely exciting; about one hundred relatives who lived in America arrived, and it took place in a large hall buzzing with interesting characters whom I had never met before.

My cousin Kevan was a similar age to me, and I got on with him well. I was impressed to hear him read in Hebrew at the ceremony in the synagogue. The afterparty was the best part, with brilliant music, dancing, and enjoyment. At the event, my brother Jonathan – who must have been about six years old – suddenly ran to the front, grabbed the microphone off the presenter, and started singing *Show Me the Way to Go Home*. Everyone fell about laughing.

I thought he was very brave for doing so in front of so many relative strangers. The whole weekend experience made me wish I was Jewish. I felt so much sympathy for how the Jewish people had suffered during Hitler's regime and the Holocaust, and I felt a real sense of belonging amongst all the lively relatives I had discovered. However, at the same time, I wondered how I would manage the strictness that Jewish traditions appeared to involve.

My dad's mother, my grandma, was quieter and smaller in stature. I do not recall what age I was, but I was given tarot cards, which I tried out with my friend Jane. The death card came up. The very next day, my grandma was hit by a vehicle in a road traffic accident and died. I was really upset, scared, and horrified by this event, and immediately threw the cards away.

My memories of early life are fragmented, partly because we moved locations a few times, and I had to keep making new friends. This left me feeling insecure and lacking a sense of belonging. My mum's parents lived in Dudley in a detached house opposite the Red Lion public house. My nana was a hairdresser, and her shop was at the bottom of their house. I recall being told by my mum's dad (Grandad) on one occasion that my mum

Mum (back row, centre right) with Laurel and Hardy, after winning a painting competition

was exceptionally talented and had won a painting competition as a child. She had met Laurel and Hardy, and he proudly showed me the photograph (previous page).

This, I thought, was in very sharp contrast to my mum's recollection of her own childhood, which she had frequently related to me was very unhappy. She told me that Grandad made her work extremely hard. My mum cited a time when she got 99% in her exams. My grandad, after hearing this good news, backed her into the corner of a room and demanded to know why she had not got 100%.

The best thing about visiting my nana and grandad was playing with my Uncle David (see photo below), their son. He used to join me on the swings and push me around in my pram. He was quiet, but I got on well with him. I always felt different and left out in my own family, but with David I had a kindred soul who understood me, and I enjoyed his company. It emerged that my grandad had been aggressive towards David, and he later

David at the family house in Sutton Coldfield

emigrated to New Zealand, partly to escape the family situation. I recall thinking that I did not blame him, and this started my desire to find a 'better life'.

I vaguely remember living in a flat near Birmingham when I was incredibly young. It was a large, open building with big rooms and a spacious garden. I was quite distressed during that time but have no idea why. Things were very unsettled. All I recall is silences between my mum and dad, which left me feeling neglected and isolated. I have memories of wetting the bed on one occasion but not really understanding why, and my parents putting something in the bed which would buzz, training me not to do it. Although it stopped quickly, I was very humiliated at the time, and can recall just wanting someone to take an interest in me. I felt very lonely.

We moved to Sheffield when I was about three years of age, due to my dad getting a job there. Growing up in Sheffield is a better memory than my early recollections of Birmingham. I really loved the place, including the Yorkshire people and their accents, the scenery, and the fact that everyone was so friendly and direct. I have always been adventurous and used to travel alone on the bus; I could go wherever I wanted to within the region. I enjoyed meeting different people and talking to them. I travelled as far as the Peak District, even as a young child, and went walking alone. I loved the way it snowed in winter, the fresh feel about it. There was often snow on the hills, which made them look so pretty. It snowed a lot in Sheffield, and I recall one day waking up and being unable to get the door open, as the snow had fallen right up to the top of our door and blocked us in. I felt incredibly pleased that I could have a day off school, as we had to wait for the snow to melt.

When I was junior-school age, we bought a house on Watt Lane in Crosspool, which caused hilarity at school as the other children would tease me, saying, '*What Lane do you live on?*' and then fall about laughing at my answer. I was certainly a tomboy and got on better fooling around with boys, who I considered my best mates. I thought at that time that boys were more exciting than girls, who always appeared serious to me. I could not see the point of dolls, although I did have a collection of teddy bears that I loved. In fact, I had so many that there was hardly any room for me in my bed. I would line them all up next to each other in a row. They were a comfort to me. They all had their own names, and I would play games with them and cuddle them at night.

I went to infant school in Crosspool, which I do not remember much about. Some boys would very insultingly do Hitler signs in front of me, due to my name being Liebling. They called me 'Leg Long Liebling', as I was particularly good at high jump. I did not mind the latter, which I took as a compliment, but I found the references to Hitler very insulting and offensive.

I took part in the high school sports each year, and although I never won, I usually did well. I was good friends with a boy called Terence, who was tall with blond hair and took a shine to me. I used to play with him on a building site and get into mischief, which I enjoyed. Terence was friendly and liked me very much, so he would make any excuse to get out of the house to see me. I liked him a lot, but always thought of him as a mate, and cannot recall if we ever kissed or anything. I remember we both used to sit on our swings and go extremely high, so that we could shout 'hello' to each other over our neighbouring fences.

When I was not at school, I spent time watching our small black-and-white television and sneaking biscuits from the kitchen in my school dress pocket. I can remember especially enjoying cowboy films.

My mum was in a bad mood sometimes and would take it out on me. However, I was extremely excited when she agreed that I could have a birthday party while we were still living in Sheffield. She complained afterwards that all my friends were boys saying, '*Why don't you know any girls?*' I laughed to myself, recalling the chaos of Lemonade and Coca-Cola going everywhere on the kitchen table while I had been joking with my male friends.

My dad had a good sense of humour about these things, although my mum was often in a bad mood with him. She smoked several cigarettes a day. However, at times, she also had a great sense of humour and was very thoughtful. For instance, one day she announced to me, 'I was thinking we should go to Betty's house'.

'I do not know. Alan Freeman's rock show is on today', I told her.

'Well, suit yourself, but it will be worth it. We could go at about two o'clock'.

'I'll think about it', I replied. I was not that interested as I did not know Betty.

'Helen, are you ready?' came my mum's voice sometime later.

'I'm coming!' I replied, now intrigued.

Later, at Betty's house, my mother introduced me to Betty.

'Pleased to meet you, Helen. Your mum said you liked cats. Come into the next room', said Betty. I instantly took to her when I saw the cat and several tiny balls of fluff.

'How brilliant! How many kittens are there? Oh, they are beautiful'.

'She had six. We are hoping to find them a loving home'.

'Mum, I love this one. Look, he is so pretty!' I pointed to a cross between a tabby and a tortoiseshell. 'Let's take him home'.

'What will we say to your dad?' my mum said, looking very worried.

'I am sure you will think of something. I am going to call him Mickey, after Mickey Mouse'.

'You can't call her that!' my mum said, laughing. 'She's a girl'.

'Well then', I said. 'I will call her Minkey'.

When we got back home, I played with Minkey until it was time for my dad to finish work. My mum said, 'We will have to hide her from your dad'.

'That's not going to be easy', I said. However, I secreted her into the attic.

Yet while we were eating dinner, my dad cocked his head and said, 'Can you hear that? It sounds as if we have rats'.

'Oh Len, you must be imagining things. I cannot hear anything', responded my mum.

'It sounds like a rat. Let me see'. My dad rushed up to open the attic door. Then he exclaimed: 'I cannot believe you have brought a kitten home. How are we going to pay for it?'

'Well, I am sure we can find the money', said my mum.

'We do not have money to pay for cat food. You will have to get rid of it'.

'No, we cannot do that. Helen loves her, and by the way, she is called Minkey', my mum replied. My dad argued, still cross. 'Fine. I will give up smoking to pay for the food, but we are keeping her', my mum finally asserted.

On days like this, I warmed to my mum, who could be truly kind. I would feel cared for. My mum and dad worked extremely hard when I was a child; in fact, I hardly saw them when we were growing up. It felt to me as though we were not close as a family, not only because my parents worked so hard but also because they expected us to do the same. I therefore relied on my friends for company and support throughout my childhood. My mum loved music and dancing, but was not a good listener, and appeared unable to hear when I was upset about something, which was distressing. I became increasingly aware that she would argue more frequently with my dad. I do not recall what the arguments were about initially, but I do remember a holiday where my dad refused to buy us more strawberries, which led to a

Me, with Minkey and my brother Jonathan

disagreement with my mother. In fact, I remember my mum thinking my dad was mean with money. I did not think he was, but at the time felt he used money to get back at my mum when she was bad-tempered with him. It felt like a dynamic that had developed due to their increasing relationship difficulties. I was closer to my dad who, although a bit distant sometimes, had a profound sense of humour and was a good listener. He loved jazz music and travelled with his friends. He was an active member of Rotary International, which I always thought was important. He was also the main member of my family who later took an interest in my work in Africa and had high morals about his actions.

My sister Ruth is eighteen months younger than me. I always felt she got on better with my mum than I did. They had more in common, being interested in cooking and shopping and being more feminine than I was. My brother Jonathan is six years younger than me, and although my sister and I had to take responsibility at an incredibly early age, I remember my mum being overprotective of Jonathan and bailing him out if he got into trouble.

In contrast, I started working at the age of thirteen to get money, as things were tough. Ruth and I work hard today; Ruth conducts research in prison and I immerse myself in fighting for the rights of people who have experienced human rights abuses – including SGBV, and those who had been tortured. Jonathan found it difficult to settle on work he was passionate about, until he started working with a mobile communications retailer and then a project using cannabis to help relieve people's medical problems.

After Jonathan was born and I was older, I remember Ruth feeling left out. Ruth became very close to Jonathan later, and then I felt left out. Although it felt to me like Ruth and my mum were closer, it was mum and I who would always go horse riding together on holidays, which I really enjoyed. I grew up wanting a horse and learned to ride at an early age, but my mum told me that a horse was too expensive. I consoled myself through weekly riding lessons, going for long rides when I could, cycling, and swimming.

My dad, who was a consultant psychiatrist, announced one day when I was about eight years of age that he had a new job, and we were moving to Sutton Coldfield. I was very unhappy and shocked about the move, which was not discussed with us. I was culture-shocked, as I loved Sheffield and felt settled with my friends. When we initially moved to Sutton Coldfield, I found the people a bit conservative. The accent appeared strange to me, as I had a strong Yorkshire accent at the time. I could not understand why people did not talk to each other on the bus as they did freely in Sheffield. I found it hard to settle and resented having to move. Although we lived in a bigger house with lovely gardens out the front and back and a nearby golf course, I would have jumped at the chance to go back to Sheffield. I missed it terribly.

Things improved when we got a dog, Sheena, a boxer who we named after the Ramones song 'Sheena is a Punk Rocker'. There was also my cat Minkey, of course. Ruth and I initially shared a room, and although we got on fine, I was glad when the house was converted, and we could move into our own small rooms.

I remember retreating to my room frequently to listen to music. Outside my room, I could see a beautiful laburnum tree with its lovely yellow blossom, and recall authoring a story about the tree at school. I was surprised and amused to learn that its incredibly beautiful flowers were poisonous.

My mum arranged for her parents, my nana and grandad, to come every Sunday. They took me and Ruth to Dudley Zoo, which was nearby. As mentioned, I got on well with David; he was a loner, and we enjoyed each other's company. We used to confide in each other and go cycling together when the family went to see my nana and grandad. On one occasion, we tried a tandem bicycle, which was great fun.

I got on very well with my nana. She was kind and thoughtful to me, and my grandad – although a brilliant pianist – would annoy me as he was sometimes critical of her. I was going through a very rebellious phase as a teenager and argued with my mum, particularly about what she considered to be my 'unsuitable' boyfriends. I recall one Sunday lunch time when I was about sixteen years of age, my grandad criticised my nana again and I had enough. I shouted and swore at him, telling him not to be so rude to her. Afterwards, my grandad sent me a letter saying he would never speak to me again. But secretly, my nana (see below), mum, and I were incredibly pleased about what I had done. I hoped he might treat my nana better in the future.

Joan, my nana

I continued to find it extremely hard to settle in Sutton Coldfield. Everyone felt more distant compared to my friends in Sheffield. I missed the cheap buses with chatty Yorkshire people, and the hills, as well as my friends. Junior school was boring to me, apart from Mr Marchant, the science teacher I fancied. I made excuses to spend time with him and ended up looking after the school's gerbils and even the salamanders, which I did not care for. It was worth it to spend time with my heartthrob; I used to enjoy getting out of French classes by telling the teacher, *The gerbils escaped!* I am not sure what it was about Mr Marchant that I found so attractive, but to me he was good-looking with a friendly but moody character, who loved animals. I was noticing the other sex more. It was much more fun to get out of lessons, which I often found boring, and spend time with him and the gerbils. My mum was annoyed when I came home at regular intervals with gerbils, especially during the holidays. They would often escape and end up in the pipes of our house, running around.

I found mischief with Ruth, who could be more serious. I do not recall how, but we found that the local YMCA had a rock disco every Friday and Saturday night. This was the most exciting thing about Sutton Coldfield. It had a non-descript door, but inside it was like a Tardis, with different rooms running off each other. It was filled with brilliant rock and punk music and interesting people. We started to make great friends, all hippies, and I constantly wore my Afghan coat, which my mother was always trying to throw away. At last, I started to fit in.

It was around this time that I really noticed my mum and dad arguing a lot. At home, my mum was upset most of the time, and my dad often appeared angry. There were frequent silences, and often my mum would be too upset to eat her food. I would finish it off, but underneath I felt distressed about what was happening. I also suspected that there was something going on I did not know about, and as usual in my family, I was always the last to know. This made the atmosphere at home very tense, and eventually Ruth told me that Mum had disclosed to her that she was 'in love with another man'. It was Eric, the married antique dealer she often visited. I do not recall at what age I found out, but I was still at junior school. I felt incredibly sad for my dad, who was such a moral man. I also felt very hurt that my mum had not told me herself.

I felt my dad took more interest in me as a child, as he listened and took me to see Aston Villa football team. I also used to cycle to see the players train at Bodymoor Heath, and got the autographs of all my favourite players, including Andy Gray and Brian Little. I recall going to see a 'friendly' at Villa Park between Aston Villa and Glasgow Rangers with my dad. When we arrived, Glasgow Rangers fans had already taken over the Holt End (the Aston Villa fans stand), and the match was stopped after two minutes due to terrible violence. Fans on both sides had invaded the pitch and furniture was being thrown around. My dad and I made a quick escape to safety. It was very scary, running away from the grounds and seeing parts of the building hurling towards us and the other Villa fans. Luckily, we fled unharmed.

The sense of isolation and loneliness stayed with me as a child. I would listen to music with my headphones on in our shared room, and sometimes I did not want to talk. I felt like a 'square peg in a round hole', and I craved my

Top left: Me; Top right and bottom right: Me with rock artist posters; Bottom left: Me and my friend Jane

own space away from the family dynamics. My sister and I had a common interest in music, and I can remember us developing a shared love of The Bay City Rollers and covering our room, even the ceilings, with their posters (see photos opposite page). I liked Eric, one of the Bay City Rollers, and my sister liked Derek. I was also 'in love' with David Cassidy and had a big poster of him by my bed, as well as another poster of David Essex. My sister had a big poster of Alice Cooper and Marc Bolan, whom she 'loved'. We even bought all the clothes and went to their concerts with our friends.

At some point, my boyfriend Patrick took me to see Be Bop Deluxe, a rock band; Ruth came along. After this, Ruth and I tore all the posters down from our room and burnt them in a bonfire, to replace them with rock band posters of Genesis, Pink Floyd, Led Zeppelin, AC/DC, and other bands we liked.

My parents really wanted me to become a medical doctor. My dad was a consultant psychiatrist, and my mum was a general practitioner. I did not fancy it much, but my parents had expectations of success, which caused me anxiety. To deal with the stress of home life, I used to spend hours riding my bicycle, hitting a tennis ball against the wall, and listening to the rock show with Alan Freeman on a Saturday afternoon. I rebelled against my parents for a sense of control in my life.

I recall Lynne, a friend from school who also studied music. Lynne's' mother took us to see Wagner, *The Ring*, a six-hour opera on one of the hottest days of summer. I was thinking at the time that I would have been content with the overture, but Lynne's mum insisted it would be good for us, since we were both studying for our O-levels in music. I also became friends with Jane, who lived across the road from me. We met at junior school and used to walk to and from school together. We stayed at each other's houses and shared midnight feasts. I remember doing a sponsored swim and spending the sponsorship money on sweets for Jane and me. Following this, one of the teachers came round to our house to claim the money and had a big argument with my mum; I do not remember his name, but his hair was red, and as he shouted at my mum about my mischief, his face turned as red as his hair. My mum told me off very harshly and made me give the money back.

Jane and I used to spend time with her brother and his friend Nathan, who I quite fancied, although they were older than us. One day they took us to Sutton Park. Jane left me with her brother, who tried to touch me, and I ran off. It was very scary, and I knew it was not right. Nathan also tried to touch me, but I managed to stop him and afterwards Jane and I decided that we were not going anywhere with them again. Jane also told me later that Nathan had tried to touch her. I do not think we ever told anybody, as we did not understand fully at the time what was happening to us. This incident left both of us feeling wary of men's intentions.

I happily passed my 11-Plus Exam, which meant I could go to the grammar school with Jane. Being a rebel, I still found myself getting into trouble. Jane was more sensible, but I also met Laura, who I called 'Drac', and we were always up to mischief. I always thought it was ridiculous how easy it was to get into trouble at school, even for writing the names of rock bands on my plimsolls or wearing badges. Drac was a tomboy as well, and we shared a similar sense of adventure. We tried to smoke once, which I did not like at all.

We also teased the teachers. Somehow, we managed to make a bomb in chemistry out of potassium permanganate, which exploded with purple smoke when the teacher came back from her break. She was not at all amused, but me and Drac laughed our socks off. One day after laughing with my friend Lynne in chemistry, I was given one hundred lines by the teacher, who asked me to write: *I will not laugh in class*. This made me laugh even more. It was a terrible thing to be told off for laughing.

The incident happened just after going to see 10cc in concert. I met Eric Stewart, the lead singer. When he signed my hand, I did not wash it for about two weeks. Lynne was great fun too, and we spent time together. She loved Ray Davies of the Kinks; we had met at the YMCA rock disco and shared a love of similar music. She took part in the Sealed Knot and was the perfect likeness of Kate Bush, which I always thought was very cool. We would stay at each other's houses overnight, and her bedroom had a grass-green carpet and walls that were painted with flowers and a rising sun. It was a great escape from the boredom of home.

At the girls' grammar school, we could not do Physics A-level for some reason, so we had to go to the boys' grammar school to study. My friends thought this was exciting, but I did not find it all that interesting. It was just a means to an end to study for my A-level. I remember this being a relief, as I did not think I had done very well in the exams after finding it hard to concentrate with my parents fighting all the time. Ruth and Jonathan went to the comprehensive school a few years later.

Things were getting increasingly difficult at home. My mum was always upset and not eating much at all. She was extremely thin. I also stopped eating well in response; I would have crackers for lunch and hardly eat in the evenings. My mum did not seem to have the capacity to think about my feelings, and I continued to rely on my friends. I recall a friend at school noticing and asking about my eating habits, but I kept the reason to myself.

Ruth, her friend Vera, and I ended up getting caught for shoplifting in a supermarket in Sutton Coldfield. We were arrested and pleaded not guilty and somehow got away with a caution. Mum and dad were furious with us.

Positively, and due to my love of music, I started playing the piano when we moved to Sutton Coldfield. I enjoyed it and would practice before school in the mornings. My love of music also helped me to express my feelings without having to say anything to anyone at home.

My mum received a present of a beautiful stand-up piano by a German doctor, who I thought fancied her. On one occasion, Jonathan – who was still a child – bashed his recorder all along the piano notes and all the keys had to be replaced, much to my mum's annoyance. I very much liked my piano teacher, a brusque Scottish woman, who was so pleased when I excelled. She entered me for a piano competition, which I did well in. My family came to see me, and my mum was immensely proud. I achieved Grade 7 and started Grade 8 but never took the examination due to the stress of home and A-levels, which I regretted. I also started clarinet at school and played in the school orchestra with my friend Lynne.

Two

Fun and Family Crises

Dinner was usually a stressful event, but on one occasion it was worse than normal. All the family took their place at the table, but before anyone could pick up their cutlery to eat, Mum directed her attention to Dad.

'I want a divorce and I want you to leave, Len. The children will stay with me'.

My eyes were immediately on my dad. His face mirrored my own horror and shock.

'Can we talk about this in private?' He asked, glancing around the table.

Dinner was ruined. I could not eat a mouthful. I later begged to live with my dad, as I felt he was more supportive of me. However, I was not given the option.

Things settled down for a while after my dad left. I then discovered the reason my mum wanted my dad out of the way. She had fallen in love with Trevor, the man she had met in the antiques shop. I had talked to him on occasion and could understand what she liked about him; he seemed kind and funny. However, Trevor was married, and although he had told my mum he would leave his wife, I felt a sense of impending doom about the relationship.

I visited them in the shop sometimes and shared my mother's delight of being surrounded by chiming clocks. Although things were more settled, I had to spend a considerable amount of time supporting my mum emotionally and looking after Jonathan and Ruth. I was thirteen years old. This put pressure on me, and I relied on my friends for support. My mum, who was often depressed and drank too much, was up and down emotionally and worked a lot to look after us. I recall her complaining about money and saying that my dad did not give her much, so she had to work hard.

One day, I returned from school to find my mum collapsed on the floor. She had overdosed.

What if she dies? I thought to myself in a panic. I felt very scared. She was taken to hospital and survived, but looked terrible. She had lost so much weight and was smoking a lot. I remember thinking that she looked like one of the starving children I saw on television during the famine in Somalia and other tragedies. I later found out that despite Trevor telling her he would leave his wife, he had – as I had suspected would happen – changed his mind. My mum fell into a terrible depression after Trevor, and when she was not working, she would listen to sad music and sob all the time. It was very upsetting. A particular favourite of hers was Nilsson's *I Can't Live if Living is Without You*. I found it all depressing. Each morning I went to school, I would wonder if she would still be alive when I returned home. For years after my dad had left and Trevor and my mum had separated, I recall her having different boyfriends, which was very unsettling for us. It seemed to me that my mum was more interested in her boyfriends than us, and I spent time looking after everyone, including my mum.

After my dad moved out, my nana and grandad took all of us – my mum, me, Ruth, and Jonathan – to Majorca, and Grandad taught me to swim. It was then that I discovered I was a 'dolphin' and the enjoyment of being immersed in water has remained all my life to the point that I still cannot resist jumping into any pool of water. I have a lot of badges for swimming and swam a mile at one point, which resulted in an award at school. Grandad taught me in the hotel swimming pool, which was surrounded by beautiful views of mountain scenery. Although it was an upsetting time, I enjoyed being by the beautiful shimmering sea, going for walks, swimming, and horse riding with my mum (see photo on opposite page). I usually got the horse that did not want to go into the sea, much to my mum's amusement. However, the holiday in Majorca gave us all the very well-earnt rest we needed. On reflection, having time with my grandparents did soften the blow of my parents break-up a little.

Whilst we were living in Sheffield, I had a friend called Audrey who lived up the road in a large house. We got on well and both shared an interest in horse riding, so she sometimes came to visit me so we could ride together. On one occasion when Audrey visited me in Sutton Coldfield, we went riding with a group in Sutton Park. It was a beautiful sunny day, and we rode by lakes and through a forest. When we were about halfway through the forest, peacefully listening to the birds, we heard a loud bang and Audrey's horse suddenly bolted off into the distance. I galloped after her through the trees and over bridges but found her fallen on the ground, upset. I called an ambulance immediately, as I was very worried about the steel plates in her hips; she was born with a dislocation. The ambulance men had to carry her in a stretcher across all the bridges in the park to the ambulance, and I

Me after horse riding in the Drakensberg Mountains, South Africa

went with her to the hospital. I was so worried about Audrey that I did not notice my own injuries, and was taken by surprise when the nurse said, *But what about you? Let me sort your face out.* It was then that I realised that I had cut my face on branches when galloping after her through the trees. We were both discharged from hospital that same day without any profound consequences, luckily.

I used to enter the 'Win a Horse' competition, which took place every week. I never won a horse, but I did win a £250 voucher. I very happily spent this at WH Smith. My mum used to say that even if I did win a horse, we would not be able to afford to keep one, which made me sad. I consoled myself by going riding as often as I was able to, and became an expert at cantering, jumping, and riding bareback. When I rode, I felt the fantastic feeling of freedom. Even Audrey's accident did not put me off.

My mum could be fun sometimes. She wanted to be 'one of us' and would take us to Rock Festivals and Barbarella's nightclubs in Birmingham when I was as young as twelve. I wore makeup so I would pass for an eighteen-year-old. She also took me to discos when we were in Majorca, but a man would always chat her up and I would feel left out. Mum took us to Knebworth rock festival and there were great bands on, including Bob Dylan and Led Zeppelin. I enjoyed the event despite being hit on the head by a cider bottle whilst hundreds of them were being thrown in the air during Robert Plant's performance of *Since I've Been Loving You*.

Whilst I was at the girls grammar school, I took a Saturday job and worked on the fish bar as well as selling the cakes on the opposite side of the counter. It was there that I met Gareth, who shared my passion for the rock band Genesis. He used to cheer up my working day by teasing me, telling jokes, and putting jelly tots on the cakes, which sophisticated women who came to the café would scowl at and insist I remove. When I looked up across the counter I would see Gareth giggling, which also gave me a laugh. Gareth was particularly good to me and wanted to go out with me, but I was hoping to start dating Patrick by then, so it never happened. I considered him a great friend. On one occasion, he drew me a pencil portrait of a Genesis album cover, which I framed; it was so beautiful.

A large part of the stress of home life whilst I was growing up, and particularly as an adolescent, was the worry of coming home from school and finding my mother had attempted suicide again. As a way of coping through the years, I went through bouts of starving myself. I found I could do this easily, and when I was working my Saturday job, I would not eat all day. I did not eat the food that was provided for us. I went out in the evenings and drank a lot at a party or at the YMCA rock disco. On reflection, I expect I drank at the weekends to be social with my friends, but also as a much needed escape from home life. I vaguely recall my mum taking me to a psychologist earlier in my life about my weight, and I was very humiliated by the whole experience. I grew up feeling sensitive about it, as my mum was always on a diet and very thin. Part of me felt like I did not wish to care, as I could not understand why my mum was so preoccupied with weight. I always felt she should be happy with how she was, and that others should be too. However, as a way of coping with the additional and unwarranted medicalisation of my distress, I started losing weight and can recall not eating at school.

The pressure from my parents to be a medical doctor was difficult for me, as I knew this was not what I wanted. I had to deal with the fallout of having my own views. The stress of home life came to a head during my A-levels when I kept fainting. We had to do dissections in biology, and there was one funny time when we were dissecting rats and the biology teacher said, *I am going out, and when I return, I want you all to have your brains out*, to which we fell about giggling. One time, we had spent all day dissecting a heart in the laboratory, which smelt terribly of formalin. Afterwards, I went home feeling very unwell, and fainted due to not eating. I told my mum it was due to the heart dissection. It was always very tricky, as my mum did not seem to have the capacity to support me since she was so preoccupied with her own life. It felt pointless telling her the truth. I consequently performed badly in my A-levels, to the disappointment of my parents, although I thought it was a miracle that I managed to pass them at all.

My mum went to see a fortune teller who had told her that she would meet a man with an accent, that my sister would be good at law, and that I would be a brilliant swimmer and talented at ballet. I remember thinking she was right about my sister, who became a professor of criminology, and about my swimming talent, but ballet was the last thing on earth I could see myself doing. Nonetheless, it gave me a smile when listening to my mum recount the story. Then, to my surprise, the fortune teller's prediction came true. My mum met an Irish man, who used to go drinking with her. I remember on several occasions cleaning up after their drunken episodes and putting my mum to bed when he had left her alone.

Luckily, the Irish man did not last long, and my mum started going out with a farmer called Donald. He was quiet and a little different, and I warmed to him. He used to take us to his farm, and I enjoyed seeing the animals there. He let me swim in his large pond, which I very much enjoyed. I got fond of him as he treated my mum a bit better than her other 'unsuitable' men. Although he was shy, I could talk to him well. One of the lambs on his farm lost her mother, so my mum offered to look after it as the other sheep had rejected it. We named her Lucy, kept her at home, and took her on leashed walks to Sutton Park to the amusement of others. When Lucy grew up, Donald said we could re-introduce her to the other sheep on the farm, which we did. We could always tell which one was Lucy, as she was the only sheep with a tail that had never been cut.

Partly to deal with my difficult and isolating home life, I started going out with boys. I had a few flings and then met Eric, who was my first serious boyfriend. He was good-looking, with an enthusiastic sense of humour, and we had similar interests. He had mousy brown hair and a nice smile. We shared a love of rock music and used to go to concerts and festivals together. I used to skive off school on a Friday afternoon with Drac, and queue for tickets at Birmingham Town Hall for rock concerts so we could get the best seats. I can recall doing this in all kinds of weather, including the snow, when I used to go into the women's toilets to defrost my hands and feet. I saw all kinds of rock bands with my friends, including Genesis, Deep Purple, Motorhead, AC/DC, Rush, Status Quo, Steve Hackett, Thin Lizzy, and Rainbow to name a few. Drac would go to a lot of concerts as well, and frequently jumped on stage. She would bring in a memento to school, like a plectrum, and give it to me as a present the next day.

One day at school, in the common room, she handed over a sorry-looking shattered guitar and announced, 'This is Ritchie Blackmore's. I got it especially for you after I jumped on stage at the Rainbow concert last night'. I thought this was hilarious, as Ritchie Blackmore was famous for smashing his guitars up at the end of his performances, and I had visions in my head of Drac pulling it off him. But I was also very touched she thought about me. On one occasion, after we had been going out for several months, Eric took me to a festival somewhere near Litchfield and brought me home late on a Sunday night. My mum went mad and hit him. Luckily, it did not put him off going out with me, although he used to be very worried about coming to our house and was incredibly nervous around my mum. We would buy each other huge cards and presents for special occasions, including birthdays, and when I ended it, Eric came to our house in an unbelievably bad mood and threw all the cards at me. I almost fell over with the weight of cards hurling towards me.

Ruth and I started having secret parties at this time, when my mum went away and left me 'in charge'. We would invite all our hippy friends from the YMCA and have a very wild time. On one occasion, one of my mum's antique tables was accidentally broken by one of my friends at a party. Whilst me and Patrick, my next serious boyfriend, had it upside down – held together with string and glue – I heard my mum's car pulling into the drive, so we frantically took the string off and put it the right way up, hoping my mum would be none the wiser. My mum noticed, and I was in trouble yet again. I always felt like the black sheep. She had split up with Donald for some reason and was in a sullen mood. I started resenting the fact that I had to look after her, when I was just a child and was getting into trouble.

I met Patrick at the YMCA rock club, and at the same time, Jane started going out with his best friend, who we affectionately named 'Big Patrick' as the four of us did a lot together. Patrick was interested in rock music too, and we went to concerts together. For my sixteenth birthday, he took me to Status Quo, and I almost got trampled to death when everyone ran to the front to be close to the stage. It was a brilliant birthday present, and I was happy with Patrick for several years. I recall a photo of me lying flat on the floor at his house the morning after I got my O-level results, as I had drunk far too much Pernod to celebrate. When I gulped a glass of water the next day, I felt drunk again and very unwell, but it was great fun.

However, after a few years, at one of the legendary parties we had at home, I opened my bedroom to see him and one of my friends, kissing. So that was the end of him. I was pretty upset by his unfaithfulness, and although he tried to plead with me, I would not take him back. He threatened to harm himself, and I felt terribly upset as I had cared very much for him. It brought up feelings of dread and reminded me of how I felt when I was trying to protect my mother from killing herself. It was like history kept repeating itself. Despite this being exceedingly difficult and traumatic for me, I stuck to my principles. By this time, Jane was going out with Carl, who she was totally in love with, so I felt a bit left out.

During our YMCA days, we were also going to Bogarts Disco in the centre of Birmingham and seeing rock bands. I found it extremely exciting going to rock concerts and festivals, including Reading Rock Festival. I used to go to the market in Birmingham to buy incense sticks and hippy clothes.

Things continued to be difficult at home as we hardly saw my dad after he left. He started going out with Margaret, an Irish woman, and they soon married. He told me he had to get permission from the Pope, as my dad was Jewish and Margaret was Catholic. On rare occasions, Margaret – who was very jealous – would let us come to her house and see our dad, but it was clear she was not that happy to have us around. We always felt in the way, and it was difficult to talk to Dad alone. Margaret had three daughters: Eleanor, Daisy, and Barbara. Barbara had meningitis when she was young, which had affected her speech and her ability to look after herself. I got on best with Daisy, the oldest of Margaret's daughters, and Eleanor was my father's favourite. We all felt pushed out.

It was around this time that my grandad had a car accident and the doctors thought he may have had a Transient Ischemic Attack (TIA). Interestingly, and to my great surprise, when my nana (see photos next page) and grandad arrived on Sunday for lunch as usual, he said, *Hi, Helen, how are you? Have you been playing the piano?* I almost fainted in shock, as this was the first time he had spoken to me in years, since I had sworn at him for ordering my nan around. He had obviously forgotten that he would never speak to me again.

Nana

One of the ways I got through these tough times was by surrounding myself with friends, partying, going out with boys, and hoping I would get into university. My parents getting divorced during my schooling impacted my studying and concentration. I had to retake my A-levels and went to college for a year to do so. I do not recall much about college, as it was not

Mum with her partner Martin

very exciting, but I got good grades when I retook my A-levels, so it did the trick. I recall eating normally again and feeling more in control of my own life, as I knew I was going to study psychology, which I wanted to do.

In about 1978, when I was seventeen years of age, Mum moved her partner Martin in to live with us at home. Mum had previously known Martin in medical school. He was divorced, and they seemed well-suited. This was a great relief to me as finally Mum had someone other than me to look after her.

Another significant event for me was my eighteenth birthday in November, 1979. Martin and Mum took me for a meal in Birmingham city centre. However, we were stopped from going into the city centre as the police said there had been an incident. We went for a meal somewhere else and then returned home. It was then that, with horror, I saw on the news that the IRA had blown up a pub in Birmingham and several people had died. I remember feeling relieved it was not us, but also very suspicious about whether it was really the IRA who had done it.

It later emerged later that there would be a great injustice, a subject that would become especially important in my life. My early life experiences shaped me into the person I became – someone who stood up for others who were badly treated, especially with a focus on gendered atrocities.

At the beginning of 1981, when I was nineteen years old, I noticed that Mum was getting fatter. This was strange, as she was usually on a diet and kept herself very thin. She told the family she was pregnant, and on July fourth, 1981, my stepbrother Philip Carmalt was born. In 1981, Ruth and I went to university at the same time – Ruth to a university in Yorkshire and me to a university in South Wales.

Martin with Phil, as a baby, at home in Barnt Green

.

Three

Adventures and Fun in Wales

I was extremely excited about going away to university. A university in Yorkshire had been my first choice, and I had a desire to return there as I had enjoyed it as a child, but when I visited the university in South Wales, I loved the fact that it overlooked the sea, so I was pleased I went there instead. The campus restaurant had huge windows that looked out on the bay, and you could see right around the coast to the lighthouse. There was something about living by the sea that was energising for me; the air was cleaner somehow, and I enjoyed the breeze and the constant changing of the sea with the weather. I was relieved to leave home and have my own independence.

I had just started going out with Dan a few months before I left. My mum liked him a lot, which I always felt was an unbelievably bad sign. She thought he was good husband material and very dependable. I had quite different taste to my mother, who liked to be looked after by men, whereas I preferred a more equal partnership. I expect my mum felt that Dan was a good influence on me as he was stable, and I was more adventurous and wilder. He went to a university up north, and we saw each other every month initially, taking turns to visit. After some time, although he treated me very well, I got bored and preferred to stay at university with my friends. Dan enjoyed a routine, and eventually the thought of living my life with such a routine filled me with dread, so I ended the relationship. Dan later started going out with Jane, my best friend from when I was younger, who I enjoyed midnight feasts with, and I always thought they were much better suited to each other than we were. They are still together, but I have lost touch with them both.

Before I left for university, one of my mum's relatives mentioned that I had a cousin, Andrew, at the same university who was studying physics, so she linked me up. I lived in a tall building on campus and spent time with Andrew; he was great at showing me around and going out occasionally, which made me feel settled quickly. However, there were still times I can recall in the early days where I felt lonely, whilst I was still getting to know people. During these times, I familiarised myself with the university in South Wales and the town of Mumbles. Mumbles is situated by the sea as you travel towards the Gower Coast. I spent time getting to know the best places to visit, including the best coffee and chip shops.

However, once I started my psychology degree, I soon made friends. In the second year, a few of us who had become good friends in the first year shared a house together – Viv, Cliff, Rowan, Mark, and me. We lived in Upper Killay, which was a fair distance from the university campus. I used to cycle into the university and back every day along the railway line and along the coast, which I enjoyed. I was also friends with Frederick, who studied zoology and wore trousers with one orange leg and one purple leg, which I liked. I felt this warm glow whenever I saw Frederick bounding towards me like 'Zebedee' in the Magic Roundabout. He was often smiling, and his trousers gave him this bright and cheery look, which would make me feel happy and lucky to know him.

Soon after I arrived in South Wales, he showed me a film about how badly battery hens were treated in the United Kingdom, and I immediately went vegetarian afterwards. The film suggested that if more people in the world were vegetarian, then there would be less starvation in developing countries. This struck a chord with me as I felt empathy for people who were living in poor countries. Growing up, I had resisted going into butchers while shopping with my mum as I hated the idea of killing animals. I only ate chicken and steak occasionally, so it was not a problem for me to become a vegetarian, which I have remained to this day.

I met Kate, an English student living in Mumbles, who I thought was brilliant. I often went to stay at her house, where she was a lodger with Ros, and we became best friends. Ros (see photo opposite page) was also lovely, a ceramics tutor for the university's Adult Education Department. and we all got on famously. Ros was in her fifties, intelligent, friendly, and fun, and had previously been married to one of the psychology lecturers at the university. I am still in touch with Ros and saw her recently in Mumbles.

Together with university friends, I always did something for fresher's week and Mark suddenly announced one day, 'I have an idea. Let us have a four-course meal on that roundabout in Swansea to raise money for rag week'.

'That sounds brilliant', I told him. 'Let us dress up. What could we wear?'

'How about school costumes?' Viv suggested.

'I think it would be fun if we all wore pyjamas', Cliff added.

Left to right: Ros and Me on a walk on the Gower Coast

'Yes', said Mark, 'that would give people in the city centre something to laugh about'.

'We could add extra things like silly hats and dressing gowns', Frederick stated.

'Brilliant', Mark said, 'let's go and liven up this town'.

We all made our way into the middle of Swansea and set a large table and chairs on one of the main roundabouts. Then we had a huge four-course meal. We dressed up in our dressing gowns and sleepwear and did not realise that the camera shop opposite was filming us. This was published in the local newspaper after causing quite a scene and a lot of interest (see newspaper excerpt next page), and the following year our picture appeared on the front of the university magazine.

Another year also for Rag Week, I dressed up as a baby, but cannot for the life of me recall why, and Mark and Frederick pushed me around in a trolley through the town centre and up and down the Swansea bypass. Other fun activities we enjoyed at university were the four-legged beer races; I used to do this with Mark and Rowan. I was in the middle of the two of them,

'Rag Week' at the University of Swansea – Back row,
left to right: Cliff, Me, Rowan, and Frederick; Front row, left to right:
Viv, pedestrian, pedestrian, and Mark.

OUT to lunch . . . it was a table with a view for Swansea youngsters Joanne Warlow and her friend Nichola Angus when they were invited to join in a rag stunt by six University College, Swansea, students who were eating their lunch (dressed in pyjamas and dressing gowns of course) in the centre of the city's Kingsway roundabout. Asked what they thought of the new open-plan restaurant the two friends agreed . . . "Well it's handy for the bus."

A local newspaper article about our stunt

tied together, and ended up closing my eyes when they had to empty their bladders. I had very sore ankles by the end of it. We came sixth one year, which I thought was excellent, and we had enormous fun in the process. I never understood why Rowan and Mark drank pints in the eight pubs we had to hop around to. I drank shots, so I did not have to use the toilet, and thought this was much more practical.

Mark was a great friend. He was very tall and slim with long blond hair and a wicked sense of humour. We shared a love of rock music and could

Left to right: Rowan, Mark, Me, Viv, and Cliff, having lunch in pyjamas during Rag Week

talk to each other easily. He was studying biochemistry in the first year at university, as I was too. At the university, everyone studied three subjects in the first year before focussing on the main topic, which for me was psychology. I was close to all my friends, but Kate and Mark were the friends I connected with best. Kate was tall and slim with long brown hair and an enthusiastic sense of humour, too. I liked the fact that she was interested in politics and concerned about fairness and equality, as I am. Kate and I used to have fun and go to music concerts, fancy dress parties, and various pubs. We would save our little money from student grants for going out by eating cheaply at the local chip shop and cooking each other meals, which consisted of lentils. We slept over at each other's houses and stayed up late in the night telling each other about our adventures.

Kate had started teaching at a very run-down school in Bridgend and used to tell me about the children *throwing planks at each other*. I used to share mine and Mark's exploits in biochemistry, which we fondly named 'bring a bottle to Biochemistry'. Whilst most of the students had lab equipment in their lockers, Mark and I had bottles of vodka and whiskey. I am not sure how we managed to finish the course without being thrown out due to our rebellious behaviour. We would spend an entire day titrating chemicals, only for Mark to throw the final product accidentally down the sink. This was then a good reason to console ourselves with a drink.

The psychology lecturers were interesting and many different characters, one of whom we called Colombo, as he looked and acted just like the television star and even smoked and wore a raincoat. It amused me when he gave us a lecture, as he looked so comical, and it made his lectures much more interesting. We were often sitting in the back row at lectures, messing around and telling jokes or recovering from hangovers from the night before. This included doing impressions of the cartoon character 'Gus Honeybun', a cartoon rabbit who used to bounce up and down. This did not go down very well with the lecturers, who would look bemused, exasperated, and irritated at the same time. We each took it in turns to leave the lectures to rehydrate after the previous night's excessive alcohol intake.

In the third year, things started to get stressful, as we all had to study for our final exams. I had to finish my research on schizophrenia. We moved into separate flats and houses; luckily, Mark and Rowan were just across the road from me. I stayed in a house with Viv and Cliff, who had started going out together by then. I had a room overlooking the university's football ground, which my friends were jealous of. I could never understand this, as I was not interested at all in Rugby.

One time, Kate and I met Mark and the others by the sea, and we all decided to strip off and run in naked. We stood beside the sea, counting down from ten to one in anticipation before dropping our towels and running as fast as we could, screaming, into the sea. Then we quickly ran out again and covered up with our towels. It was hilarious and very refreshing. In the summer months, we would stay down after the university term had ended for a few extra weeks and go to our favourite beaches, including Three Cliffs and Rhossilli Bay.

When I returned home after my exams, my mum exclaimed, *My goodness, where have you been? You are so brown. You look like you have been to the South of France!* She told me she and Martin would visit for my graduation.

I always thought Mark and I would end up going out together, as he and his partner were often arguing, but it was Marcus who I became closer

View from my window overlooking the Rugby grounds at the university in South Wales

with towards the end of university. He was majoring in biochemistry, tall and slim with dark curly hair. He was an excellent saxophone player, which added to the attraction due to my love of music. He shared my fondness of swimming, too. We started going out with each other in the final year and planned a trip hitching to France after university ended in 1984.

I was incredibly pleased to get a high 2:1 for my degree and stayed in Swansea to attend graduation with my friends. One of my lecturers told me I closely missed a first-degree award, which was rewarding but also a bit frustrating. I was incredibly happy to get a 2:1 as I had a lot of fun during my time at university, and although I worked hard, I balanced my enjoyment as well. At the graduation ceremony, Francis got so drunk that he fell asleep. Half of the ceremony was in the Welsh language, so it was a challenge and difficult to follow at times. It was a very windy day, and my hair was exceptionally long then. I can recall my family and friends taking photos of me smiling with my hair flying about all over the place. The ceremony took place in the Brangwyn Hall, a very smart hall by the sea. I was incredibly happy.

My mum, Martin, Ruth, and Jonathan came down to Swansea to celebrate with me and we all went for lunch before the ceremony. I was immensely proud when I went onto the stage to collect the certificate. Although I knew I would be incredibly sad to leave, as I had enjoyed my time there and had started to feel settled, I genuinely felt university had changed me as a person. It had opened my eyes up to new and exciting experiences and broadened my interests, as well as made me excited about my future life, which I hoped would include becoming a health visitor or a clinical psychologist. Although I was not sure which profession I might prefer, I was happy enough to keep my options open at this stage.

Left to right: Jonathan, me, Ruth, and Martin in Swansea for my graduation in 1984

Four

How Far Can You Travel with £70 and a Tent?

I returned home briefly after university finished and arranged with Marcus to start our adventure. This was not as straightforward as I had hoped, as he decided to go his own way and meet me in Paris. I was annoyed and disappointed about this initially, as I had hoped we would travel together. However, it was the start of our adventure, so I let it go, thinking, *Nothing seems straightforward with him*. He made up for it by being good company and fun.

Marcus was good-looking: very slim with long black hair worn in a ponytail. Women fancied him, so I felt pleased it was me he was going out with. He came from a rich family in Surrey with a huge house, set in a huge garden and with a swimming pool. I liked the sense of its old country style with lovely wooden beams. I enjoyed the novelty of this, but I also found it all a bit outside my comfort zone. However, Marcus made me feel welcome. His father was also a famous saxophone player.

Getting ready to go travelling with Marcus

Shortly before we set off, I can remember my mum saying to Marcus, *You will look after her, won't you?* *More likely to be the other way round*, I thought, as I had already sensed I was the more practical, caring, and organised of the two of us.

The day of excitement came, and I flew with Ruth to Paris and stayed with a friend of hers, Alain, while waiting for Marcus to arrive. When he did not appear on the day we had planned, I started to get worried. I wondered whether something had happened to him. Despite this, I continued having fun with Ruth, Alain, and his family, exploring Paris for the first time. I loved going up the Eiffel Tower, despite the fierce winds. It felt scary, but I loved the sense of height and the beautiful views. I was the only person to brave the very top and felt that I and the woman selling postcards might be catapulted right across Paris into the sea by the wind.

One day, the doorbell rang, and there Marcus was looking bedraggled and pale on the doorstep. He had been missing for several days, so it was a relief to finally see him. I barely had time to ask him how he was before he fell on the floor in front of me. I realised he had fainted, which scared me. When he came round, he told me what had happened:

'Well, I hitched to Dover, got on the ferry, and met this Scottish bloke. We got chatting, and he had a bottle of Vodka, so we drank the whole lot, and I do not know what happened but when I woke up, he had stolen all my possessions, including our tent. It was then that I realised he must have hit me over the head with the Vodka bottle and knocked me out, so when I reached France, I had to have stitches in the hospital'.

Although I was sympathetic, I thought this could be an omen. I had set off on the journey with high hopes and on reflection this was a warning sign. We had started our hitching adventures with £70, a recorder, and a tent between us, and now we only had £50 and no tent. After Marcus had rested, we started off and hitched a ride very easily from Paris. A man picked us up who was on his way to Carcassonne, so we just went with the flow, and I jumped in beside him. At the time I was not even sure I knew where Carcassonne was. He was an interesting travel companion but a little strange, I thought. Nevertheless, I sat in the front, and we chatted away while Marcus slept in the back. He was still recovering from the head injury incident and not yet quite himself.

I cannot recall why I thought the guy who picked us up was a bit strange. He was very friendly, which inspired confidence, but a bit overfamiliar in his manner. I was a bit cross with Marcus for falling asleep and leaving me alone with this man. *What if something happened?* I thought to myself. *Marcus would be none the wiser.* His strangeness became confirmed in my mind when about halfway into the journey he offered to take a photo of us both. He asked for my address, which I gave him mainly because I really wanted a copy of our photo. Although afterwards, I did wonder if I had made a mistake in giving him my personal details.

However, true to his word, about one year later an envelope appeared in the letterbox, and sure enough there was the photograph of Marcus and I. As expected, it was strange. The photo was of me and Marcus in the front, and then another couple in the background. I assumed the unusual driver had given a lift to another couple and superimposed our pictures.

When we reached Carcassonne, we found a campsite and bought a small stove. I thought Carcassonne was beautiful, with its lovely buildings and the huge castle overlooking it. We went to a bread shop, and the women behind the counter took one look at the skinny, exhausted Marcus before kindly giving us all their leftover bread. He seemed to bring out motherly instincts in women, including me, although it was starting to get a bit annoying as I also wished to be looked after. As we were doing well, we then visited the Cave Co-operative, and the manager kindly gave us free wine. Most nights, we had lentils with marmite and bread with copious quantities of red wine. *Not bad for free*, I thought.

However, we soon realised we would run out of money, as £50 does not go far in France. Besides, we had to buy another tent. After buying the tent, we had about enough for a couple of meals and then we would be struggling. I suggested to Marcus that we go busking at Carcassonne Castle to earn more coppers. I started playing my recorder, which I had very sensibly packed, and got a bit of money from blowing out Beatles tunes and anything else I could remember from my school days. I could not believe it when Marcus started playing the recorder and everyone who passed donated to him. We earnt about £20 a day. I rolled my eyes, thinking, *Amazing. At least there are some advantages to his condition.* We happily ate and drank very well for several days on our earnings, which we topped up with free wine and bread.

After about two weeks, we realised that busking was not very sustainable, and besides, we wanted to travel a bit more. So, we hitched and got a ride to the north of France. I cannot recall exactly where, but we pitched our tent at night, and in the morning, we woke to a lot of car noise. When I went outside, I realised we had somehow camped on a busy island in the middle of a road junction. We hastily packed up our meagre belongings, feeling very amused that we had managed to sleep our way through the 'rush hour' of French traffic.

The next person who gave us a lift dropped us off near a wine farm in Bordeaux. We went to offer our services for grape-picking and quickly got a job, which was exciting. *Our first proper job*, I thought to myself, feeling incredibly positive. It was brilliant fun, as we camped in the garden and had all our meals included, plus as much wine as we could drink. Although it was red wine and my preference was always for white, I did not complain.

The grape-picking was extremely demanding.

The work involved crouching opposite each other on our knees and cutting the grapes whilst trying hard not to cut each other's fingers off. At regular intervals, the harvest was suddenly halted by the farmer as someone had left their secateurs (clippers) in the basket, and it would block up the grape-smashing machine. It was tiring work, but we were happy to have a job for two weeks. During the second week, I went to go to the bush toilet and was very shocked to see the main farmer with his trousers down, exposing himself in front of me. I felt very frightened and vulnerable. I knew that even if I screamed, we were far away from the others, and I was unlikely to be heard. I walked off, feeling disgusted, but also used my sense of humour to laugh about it with Marcus later.

The incident really affected me hugely, though, and I kept my distance from the farmer. I could not wait to receive our monthly earnings so that we could leave the place. I reflected positively on our busking, thinking that this was a safer option for getting money. I do not think Marcus really understood the gravity of the situation, and although concerned for my welfare, he did not appear to pay much attention to it. His response was disappointing. Despite finding it slightly amusing myself, it had really upset and angered me, and it brought home to me how vulnerable such acts can make young women. On top of incidents that had happened earlier in my life, the incident provoked strong feelings of injustice, and made me determined to fight for the rights of survivors of SGBV and other abuses. I used my humour and resilience to deal with the incident, but at the same time, I knew it was time to leave. I had had my fill of red wine, which was not worth the situation I found myself in.

Having earnt money grape-picking, we decided to take the bus to Athens. I do not recall this journey very well, as I mostly slept. When we arrived, we camped on a very stony campsite with very thin carry-mats. I enjoyed being in Greece – the blue skies and sea, warm sun, and beautiful scenery. We went to see the Parthenon and other historic buildings. When the sunset lit the Parthenon up at dusk, it turned a beautiful bright colour against the red sky and looked wonderful.

I discovered that we could get an unbelievably cheap boat if we sat on the top deck from Haifa to Israel. It did not take much persuading for Marcus to agree to buy tickets. After a few days, we boarded for Israel with a tent, a bit of food, and not much money at all. I was very aware that we did not have a job to go to in Israel, but we were extremely excited all the same.

The three-day boat journey was fabulous, and we met other adventurous hippies going to work in Israel, on a Kibbutz. We stopped at Cyprus and Rhodes and were able to have time to explore them and swim. On a very sunny day, I was looking at the sparkling blue sea when I suddenly saw a pod of dolphins spinning and jumping their way alongside the bow of the boat; it was so beautiful, and I called Marcus over. We excitedly watched them, feeling like we were in heaven.

We arrived in Israel, and at customs an austere-looking man asked us if we had work. I had to react quickly, so I showed him my bank card and said we had enough money to live on. Amazingly, he let us in the country.

We went to an office in Tel Aviv and found we could work on a Moshav farm or a Kibbutz. The woman we were speaking with informed us that there was room for me and Marcus to work on a Moshav about one hundred kilometres north of Eilat. We gladly took the opportunity and made our way to the Moshav, where we were greeted by a very stern-looking man who showed us a room in his garage where we could stay.

The stern man, who was unfortunately to be our boss, informed us that we would work every day on the farm starting at 3 a.m. due to the heat. We could take food from the farm to eat, and he would give us a loaf of bread each day. We later discovered that this was sensible advice, as tourists were frequently found almost dead on the road from heat exhaustion after experiencing the midday sun. We started work the next day, and I felt exhausted after an hour. *Goodness*, I thought to myself, *I don't know how I am going to manage this*. We picked tomatoes, onions, peppers, aubergines, and flowers. I enjoyed picking the flowers. It was the most comfortable job. We picked a beautiful variety of flowers called Gypsophila, small white flowers with long green stems. They were easy to cut, and I found it relaxing. We then stored the flowers in a large fridge, so that they would not open until they arrived in Europe. They remain one of my favourite flowers to this day.

The farmer thought that Marcus was trustworthy, but that I was not at all. I thought this was very chauvinistic, since Marcus was a man, and he would do the work well. As I was a woman, he must have thought I needed supervising. I found this highly insulting. He followed me everywhere, checking that I had picked all the tomatoes. I would try to reassure him that I was doing an excellent job, but eventually would sigh to myself. I hoped he would notice and stop doing it, but my actions were to no avail. It was very off-putting. It all seemed particularly unfair and sexist, as I was also the one who knew how to drive the tractor. I felt incredibly angry and irritated by the farmer's treatment and attitude towards me, and I felt deeply sorry for what I suspected was his long-suffering wife. On Fridays, his wife would invite us over for food with their family. She was very friendly and cooked us falafels, which I loved, although I found it hard to watch her being ordered around by the farmer.

One day, the farmer took us out to one of the melon fields after the harvest and went up and down with the tractor. Then he announced to us, 'Right, I want this field cleared by the end of the morning'.

'I trust you will leave us the tractor', I responded to deaf ears, slightly worried about the task ahead, to which he replied, 'No, you just use your hands'. It was very exhausting, but about two days later – much to the farmer's annoyance – we had cleared the field with our hands. I was sure he expected that I was not capable of it, and this made me more determined to prove him wrong.

The farm was in the middle of the desert, and there was not much to see. Marcus and I would go for walks, but we had started arguing and getting on each other's nerves. This was not good as we spent so much time together. The fun of the previous adventures had worn off, and Marcus upset me. I became so distressed that I started harming myself with my pen knife to express my feelings. I cannot recall well what made me think of doing this, but I was aware of building feelings of neglect, and a lack of attention and care from Marcus. I had a dislike of confrontation from an early age, as it reminded me of my parents arguing. So, trying to 'have it out' with Marcus did not seem a viable option. Underneath, I realised it would not get me anywhere. However, I also felt some sense of relief after doing it, which surprised me, but gave me the immediate calm I needed. It also enabled me to find my voice in some way. I hoped that he might treat me better, but it did not produce the response I desired.

The isolation of where we were working made the situation difficult. I had no mates to sound off to about the situation, and Marcus seemed to have stopped listening. This set up a terrible pattern of him continuing to upset me, and things got worse. The way he sided with the stern man also irritated me, as I felt he really should defend me. I got into a pattern of going for a walk and sometimes harming myself whenever he upset me. I realised the self-harm was a way to express the anger I was feeling towards Marcus and to help me communicate in a situation where I was not being listened to. Eventually, I managed to stop myself from doing it and just went for long walks to let my anger out. This tricky situation enabled me to take control of my own destiny, turning me into a resilient survivor.

The highlight of our week was getting the farm transport to the only shop for miles, and only one of us could go so we took it in turns. On my birthday in November, we treated ourselves to a chocolate cake which we ate in about ten minutes, as we were so hungry. I have never eaten a cake so quickly in my life. I had the brilliant idea to go and stay in Eilat to celebrate for the weekend. Having little money, we slept on the beach with our sleeping bags and the rats for company. I loved the freedom and the chance to visit the underwater observatory and see all the colourful fish. It was my idea of heaven, and Marcus was in a good mood.

After my birthday, things deteriorated further. I was feeling homesick and really wanted to go home for Christmas. We had earned a fair bit of money, so we returned to Eilat and enquired about flights to the UK for Christmas and managed to book two one-way charter flights to return on Christmas Eve. This eased the pressure on both of us, and we spent our last weekend visiting the Dead Sea. The sea was beautiful, a very deep blue. We bobbed about on the water, which was great fun. The large volume of salt in the water made us very buoyant, and you could almost sit upright in it. It was a welcome break after all the stress. On Christmas Eve, we flew back to the UK and Marcus went off to Surrey. I returned to my mum's and step-father's house.

Five

Tropical Snorkelling, Personal Dilemmas and Navigating High Security

'What's that?' Mum asked.

I quickly skimmed the letter and replied, 'It is good news, Mum. I have a place to do nursing in Birmingham'. However, I was also thinking to myself how disappointed my mum seemed that I had not wanted to become a medical doctor.

I managed to find a room in a house in Balsall Heath and Marcus got a place to study for his PhD in Belgium. I was apprehensive about this, as we were already having problems and I was concerned the distance would make things worse. I was also still unsure that the relationship was right for me. I visited Marcus a couple of times in Belgium, but it was hard as he had clearly moved on with his life. He seemed close to two women friends, which was difficult, and they were very motherly towards him. He neglected me, as he had in Israel.

One morning, I woke up feeling extremely sick, and knew I had missed a period. *Oh dear*, I thought to myself and went off to Boots to get a pregnancy test. I returned home, did the test, and then waited with anticipation. As I watched the test turn to positive, I felt a huge sense of panic. *Now what?*

Although I was ambivalent about it, I eventually told Marcus. He did not appear to be interested in having a child. I agonised about what to do, and eventually, although it was hard, I decided due to Marcus' lack of interest, and the distress he had caused me, to have an abortion. I did not want to bring up a child alone. This was much more difficult than it seemed initially, and although I thought I had made the right decision, I was very depressed for about eighteen months afterwards. It was as if I felt how the baby must have been feeling. I cried a lot of the time. Marcus and I also finished around the same time, and this made things even more difficult. Again, I felt very isolated.

Luckily, Kate, who I had kept in touch with since university, lived in the house. We got on very well, although she was in a relationship with Bertie, so I did not spend as much time with her as I would have liked. After some flirting and good times, I had a brief relationship with Eric, who lived down the road, but we both knew it was nothing serious. He had an infectious personality and strong political views, and was not afraid to speak his mind, which I liked. He was a keen cyclist, and I would often turn up at his house to find him going 'hell for leather' on his bicycle, which was fixed to the floor in his lounge. I was acutely aware that I was on the rebound from what had happened with Marcus and wanted a distraction to numb the hurt. Having said that, I really liked Eric.

I also found nursing difficult, as my view was nurses were not treated with the respect they deserved. When I asked questions about open heart surgery while working in theatres, I got told off. In fact, I spent most of my nursing career getting into trouble for 'fooling around'. I knew I was a great nurse and particularly good at listening to the patients. I found this period of my life difficult, as underneath I was aware that nursing was not right for me. The personal distress of my recent break-up with Marcus, in addition to the impact of having an abortion, was extremely hard to deal with. It was made more bearable by having fun. A staff nurse when I was working nights would crack a lot of funny jokes on the medicine rounds and have me and the patients in stitches. She put a blow-up reindeer on the medicine trolley whose nose lit up, and this caused great hilarity. The fun really helped manage the pain I was going through at the time.

I developed a good friendship with another one of the nurses, who I later went inter-railing with. That was a wonderful experience, and we travelled all though France, across Germany, and into East Berlin, as well as to former Yugoslavia. The trip into East Berlin particularly sticks in my memory as it resonated with my dad's Jewish roots. I was horrified by the Nazi-looking guards with guns who strutted across the rail lines. It gave me a sense of foreboding and horror. Looking around the remains of East Berlin felt to me like going back in time. There were old broken-down cars, small houses, and extreme poverty. After a while, we decided to get something to eat. We went to a restaurant and sat down to eat what looked like pickled cabbage as there was not much choice for vegetarians. Two men came and sat next to us. They related their situation; they were trying to get back to their families in West Berlin and wanted us to help get them out. I felt so upset and helpless when we left, as I really wanted to help them. Many years later after the Berlin Wall had fallen, I returned to Berlin for a conference. I went to a black-and-white photograph exhibition on the border of East Berlin and seeing the photographs brought back the memories very strongly.

After I qualified as a nurse, I worked as a staff nurse for six months at a central hospital in Birmingham on a 5-day surgical ward. I had bought a motorbike and had a lot of fun riding it, much to my mother's displeasure. I had a friend who had a huge Honda motorbike and she used to take me on long rides. I loved the freedom that the bike gave me.

After a few months of working as a nurse, I realised I still wanted to be a clinical psychologist. I started applying for jobs and was incredibly pleased to be offered a job as an assistant psychologist at a high-security hospital. Following the initial excitement, I felt apprehensive about getting the job, as I knew the hospital was where Ian Brady and Peter Sutcliffe, the serial killers, were held.

Peter Sutcliffe was an English serial killer who was named the 'Yorkshire Ripper' by the press. On 22 May 1981, he was arrested in Sheffield and found guilty of murdering thirteen women, as well as attempting to murder seven others between 1975 and 1980. Ian Brady was born in Glasgow, Scotland, and as a teenager spent time in young offenders' institutions. He met Myra Hindley while they were both working together in Manchester. They carried out the Moors murders between July 1963 and October 1965, in and around Manchester. Five children were murdered, at least four of whom were sexually assaulted. One of the victims' bodies has still not been found. I wondered what I was doing.

However, I consoled myself with the fact that it was a means to an end, and the experience would surely give me a good chance of getting onto clinical psychology training. About a month before I started my role at Broadmoor, my mum announced, 'You can have my car for your job if you promise to get rid of that motorbike, Helen'.

'That's brilliant, Mum, but I want to keep the motorbike as well'.

'That is the deal, Helen. If you do not sell the motorbike, I am afraid I cannot give you the car. You know it is the sensible thing to do as you need a car for your new job'.

Reluctantly, I came to the decision that it made sense to take my mum's offer of her car, although I was very unhappy about selling my motorbike. My mum's car was a blue Beetle which I loved. I sadly knew I could not afford to buy a car myself, and I did need one for my job. The whole situation made me very resentful of her and the power she had over me. I would be living in the flats at Broadmoor Hospital and working in it, so I wondered how much I would really use a car. However, I knew it would give me the independence I desired.

The day came when my mum escorted me to the motorbike shop, and I was terribly upset about selling it. I almost burst into tears when I left it at the shop, but my mum was incredibly happy when I did. This made it worse. I moved to Crowthorne and stayed in the nurse's residence. I was isolated and I felt cut off from the rest of the world. I shared a flat with a quiet woman who also worked at the hospital and practiced Thai Chi, but she did not talk to me very much. I started going out with one of the nurses at the hospital, and this helped as I did not feel so isolated and lonely anymore.

When I first arrived at the high-security hospital and saw the huge buildings with immense security and big gates, I felt a sense of trepidation. Despite my reservations, I soon settled into the job and started enjoying it. I felt safe in my role and enjoyed the large gardens where some of the patients worked. I also liked the workshops, particularly the bookbinding and carpentry shops, as they gave the hospital a sense of being a huge village of which I was a part. The carpentry staff and patients were happy to make me a rocking horse for my younger brother, Phil, and I was so thrilled the day I picked it up. The patients who had made it also shared in my excitement. They were proud of their work, and I was grateful for it.

In spring, the smell of freshly cut grass and spring flowers made the hospital feel bright and cheery, and the staff and patients were mostly good-humoured. I soon fit into the culture. I worked for four different clinical psychologists, which was interesting as I saw both male and female patients. It was a particularly valuable experience, and I knew it would help me get on the clinical psychology training course. I recall feeling more comfortable with the women patients but enjoyed all my work and found it very stimulating. I met a music therapist who worked in the hospital, who I got on with well. I worked with a famous psychotherapist and enjoyed how challenging the work was. Some of the male patients would make me laugh by telling me about one psychiatrist who used to fall asleep in their therapy sessions. Although funny, I felt angry that a professional could get away with such behaviour.

I worked with a male psychologist who worked with sex offenders and used a behavioural technique that involved showing images and measuring the erection. He was successful in his work, but I felt a bit nervous about the behavioural approach used, and preferred talking therapies. I was keen to understand the reasons why patients were in the hospital in the context of their life experiences and wanted to provide therapy in a non-judgemental way. I recall Jimmy Savile coming into the hospital and remember thinking that it was very strange he had such easy access compared to the staff. I recall him wearing his gold Lurex suit, but I did not meet him. Years later, when the abuse allegations emerged, it sadly did not surprise me.

I got on particularly well with Christine, one of the clinical psychologists, who worked at the hospital. One weekend, we travelled down to enjoy a folk festival in Sidmouth in her Citroen 2CV. We had great fun. I soon got bored with living in Crowthorne, so decided to join the scuba diving club in Reading. I was learning to dive in the swimming pool and instantly got on with a fellow student called Clarissa. She was also learning to dive and studying for her BSc in Genetics at university, and we became great friends. Things improved, as often at weekends I would stay over at Clarissa's house, or we would go away on diving trips. Clarissa and I shared similar interests and an enthusiastic sense of humour, so life was good again.

There were several parties during this time, and I remember us dancing wildly to music, including the Communards and Blues Brothers. There was a guy I had dived with called Craig who was a little strange, but I found him fun, and we started going out together. He was quiet, but had a very dry sense of humour, and we also dived together quite a bit. I learnt a lot from him, and my diving skills really improved. I knew he fancied me, as he made suggestive comments towards me. At the time, I found it funny, although in retrospect I think this could have been a warning sign.

Left to right: Clarissa and Me snorkelling in Belize

Clarissa and Me in Belize

One weekend, I was due to go on a diving trip in Scotland to the Isle of Mull. When I left the flat, four of us were in the car, and it was about 4 a.m. in the morning. The sky was still dusky. Suddenly, as if out of nowhere, a police car came speeding towards us the wrong way down a one-way street and we had a head-on collision. All I remember is seeing blood as my head smashed the side window; I was sitting on the back seat. I was scared, as I thought I had cut my eye open. The ambulance took us all to hospital. The two people in the front ended up with whip lash, but I had to get stitches above my eye and still have the scar unfortunately. The guy sitting next to me fell forwards, smashed into the front seat, and damaged his sight permanently, which was awful. We still left for the diving trip the following day, but I felt sick and dizzy and suffered from concussion. Sometime later, we sued the police, who stated in court that they were responding to an emergency call out. However, we won our case and the police paid damages, although the pay-out did not make up for my permanent scar and the loss of my friend's sight.

After this incident, I became even more worried about Craig, as he started to do things that scared me. He followed me on a train when I ended the relationship. I was so frightened that I jumped off the train and ran to the nearest police station, but it was late, and the police scared me too; they were both men. I went back to my mum's and stepdad's house and remember feeling as though my parents did not seem to believe me. My dad wanted me to see a psychiatrist. I was horrified by this and found it very insulting. I was particularly annoyed by my father, pathologising what I considered a normal emotional reaction to a traumatic situation. It was very disappointing as I was closer to my dad, and this made it worse. What I had wanted was a validation of my experiences.

Luckily, soon after this incident, I learned that I had secured a place at university to study clinical psychology and started the position of trainee clinical psychologist. I was not sorry to leave Crowthorne at all but was incredibly sad to leave Clarissa. However, she would be moving to the United States to study for her master's degree, and I felt extremely excited about moving to Edinburgh.

Six

A Scottish Journey into African Music

When I initially moved to Edinburgh, I shared a flat near one of the parks. The building was beautiful and had a magnificent view, and I fell in love with Edinburgh very quickly. I loved the tall buildings, the surrounding hills, the liveliness of the city, as well as being close to the sea. I really enjoyed being in a different place, which made it remarkably interesting and exciting. I shared the flat with a woman who I got on well with, and who was also studying clinical psychology, the same course as me. I had been interviewed by a health authority in the Midlands for the place on the Scottish training course, although I found it strange that the training was in Scotland and not nearer to the Midlands. I started the course and the ten of us enrolled soon got to know each other. I attended lectures and my first placement, and I soon made friends to socialise with.

I got to know Andy during a skiing trip. I noticed him when he was laughing his head off about something and was instantly attracted to him. We soon started going out; I was the happiest I had been in ages, and we got on brilliantly. He was incredibly supportive and fun to be with. There were a lot of parties and some cannabis smoking, although my hard partying did not affect my coursework, as I stubbornly ensured my reading and essays were up to date. I also got on well with the service users I worked with on different placements, and therefore passed them all.

Andy was born in Uganda, whilst his parents were working there at Kyambogo College in Kampala. Unfortunately, they had to leave when Andy was three years old, due to Idi Amin and the resulting instability.

Idi Amin Dada Oumee, who died in 2003, was a Ugandan military officer and politician who served as the third president of Uganda from 1971 to 1979. He ruled as a military dictator and is considered one of the most brutal dictators in modern world history. During his years in power, Amin shifted from being a pro-Western ruler enjoying considerable support from Israel to being backed by Libya's Muammar Gaddafi, Zaire's Mobutu Sese Seko, the Soviet Union, and East Germany. He also expelled all Asian people in 1972, the majority of whom were Indian Ugandans. Otherwise, Amin's rule was characterised by rampant human rights abuses, including political repression, ethnic persecution, and extrajudicial killings. Human rights groups estimate that between 100,000 and 500,000 people were killed under his regime.

Andy and I shared a love of music, and he started teaching me Ugandan instruments including ngoma (drums), amadinda (wooden xylophone), endongo (thumb piano), and endingidi (tube fiddle). In the second year, our relationship was going so well that we made a joint decision to move into a flat together. I was really delighted about this as it felt as though we were soul mates.

Once Andy and I were established in our new accommodation, we continued to have parties. I recall one where we all dressed up as characters from 'Alice in Wonderland'. I went to the party as the Mad Hatter, wearing many watches on my jacket, and a friend was the Queen of Hearts, carrying her heart on a stick. Andy and his friend dressed up as Tweedledee and Tweedledum and had pillows stuck up their jumpers to make them more realistically fat. Laura, another friend, was the dormouse, and we had several other characters. In the kitchen, we had a long table set out like the Mad Hatter's tea party as it was recounted in the book, except instead of tea in the pot we had punch. It was great fun. I loved spending time with Andy, drumming, talking, and going walking on Arthur's Seat – or 'Arthur's Rabbit' as we fondly called it. We thought it looked more like a rabbit or an

Andy and Me at his parents' house in Sutton Coldfield, 2021

elephant when you looked at it from a distance. We also went further afield, including to the Scottish islands, where we would camp at folk festivals, sell cakes, and play Ugandan xylophone to earn some money. This went down well with the festival goers, who were fascinated by the instrument and gave their money generously. We made over £200 during a weekend festival. It meant that we could afford to eat and live well, without having to scrounge off our friends or Andy's parents.

I enjoyed my placements while training, particularly one in the borders, as my supervisor was great. He was very friendly and frequently took me for tea and scones. He was a relaxed father figure who liked me, and I felt extremely comfortable with him. He negotiated my work experience and enabled me to have flexibility. We worked in a big psychiatric hospital, but all the staff and patients were very sociable, and I felt very settled.

I had a challenging supervisor in Falkirk, so did not enjoy that placement much. He was curt in his manner and did not seem to have the warmth that neglected children required from their professionals. I loved working with the children, but my feelings about the supervisor spoiled the enjoyment of my work.

My last placement was in a women's prison in Scotland. I had a brilliant woman supervisor there, which was a complete contrast to my previous experience. My skills were recognised and further developed. I carried out my research with women who self-harmed at the prison and did a comparison at a women's hostel in Glasgow. I was based at a Forensic Unit in Glasgow and worked at a men's prison there, although I was not there long after some riots. I spent some of the time speaking to prison officers who had been affected, as well as prisoners. As David Cook wrote (1991):

'On the afternoon of January 5, 1987, violence erupted in B hall in Barlinnie Prison. A number of officers were trapped in cells, and the inmates demolished the facilities in the hall. Fires were started as the inmates tried to smoke out the officers who had been trapped in the cells. Many of these officers thought they were going to die. Three prison officers were taken hostage by eleven inmates. The incident continued for approximately four days. The Barlinnie riot was only one in a series of riots and hostage-takings that occurred in Scottish prisons in the late 1980s. Inmate hostility continued after the riot ended. The author, who is a psychologist on the staff of the Greater Glasgow Health Board, received many of the referrals of prison officers suffering from psychological problems following this period'.

According to the *Daily Record* (2012), an insider said: *The riots were not caused by brutality from warders or the harsh regime. They were caused by men who live by violence in or out of prison.* John Renton, head of the Scottish Prison Officers Association, blamed overcrowding, and understaffing.

The riots affected the relationships between prison officers and prisoners, with the balance of power shifting to the prisoners. Officers felt very threatened and de-skilled. I could really understand the situation, feeling by then that only therapeutic approaches worked for people who ended up in prisons. I enjoyed those placements, loved forensic work, and found it remarkably interesting and challenging.

When I finished the clinical psychology course and graduated, I obtained a job in a Scottish prison and drugs centre but was supposed to return to the Midlands to work. I felt very settled in Edinburgh, and as I was going out with Andy, I arranged a meeting with the Health Authority to let them know I would prefer to stay in Edinburgh. I was happy that they agreed to let me work in Scotland, as I could stay closer to Andy. Initially, I tried to commute from Edinburgh, but it was very tiring, and I ended up sharing a flat in Dundee to save time and energy. It was a terrible wrench moving away from Andy, but deep down I felt I had no other choice than to move. On reflection, it was likely this was a misjudgement on my part.

I enjoyed my work and did not consider that anything could go wrong. However, I noticed after about nine months that the other two psychologists at the prison, who were good friends, started treating me differently. At first, I thought it was my imagination, but as the weeks went on, I was sure I was right about their ill will towards me. I talked to Andy about it, and he thought it must be jealousy. I had a particularly good relationship with the governor of the prison, who at the start of my role had sent me to San Francisco to learn about sex offender treatment programmes, which he wanted to be available in the prison. If Andy was right, then this would have made their jealousy worse. Things started to become difficult for me as I was popular in the prison, worked hard, and was getting on very well with the prisoners and other staff members.

After I had been working for eighteen months, I went to speak to a manager of the service, who was sympathetic until I mentioned the names of the culprits. Then I could sense he was unwilling to help me sort the problem out. He was at the same time patronising and flirtatious with me, and suggested I should 'just forget about it'. This really annoyed me. I felt stuck in an exceedingly tricky situation in terms of the power dynamics of these relationships. Things got increasingly difficult, and I plodded on, trying to ignore the situation until the two women in the prison had me suspended. They had complained about me to the lead clinical psychologist with 'made-up' allegations. I do not recall the detail of their complaints, but I felt they 'were out to get me' from the very start. I felt victimised by their behaviour towards me, which was grossly unfair and unjust. I was upset, angry, and fearful of losing my employment. As a woman and a feminist, having two women gang up against me and get a male manager on their side was very disappointing to me. The situation the women created meant I had to employ the services of a lawyer in Edinburgh. This caused the atmosphere to become worse, as the women in the service became even more aggressive towards me. The cost of the legal services was high, although it was worth it to have such good advice and representation. The situation went on for months and was incredibly stressful. I remember Andy being brilliant during this time and incredibly supportive. He attended all the appointments with the lawyer with me and spent hours helping me prepare for difficult meetings.

Andy and Me playing Amadinda (Ugandan xylophone) for Amnesty International in Liverpool

My woman lawyer in Edinburgh was very professional and thorough, and we won the case without going to a tribunal. By this time, I had decided to leave as the atmosphere was so awful. It felt very unfair and unjust that untrue allegations could result in my having to leave employment I had enjoyed and been successful in. It did knock my confidence, but my lawyer assured me that I would have a good reference and be able to get another job. I was determined to get better employment afterwards.

Andy playing the *adungu* (Ugandan harp)

I moved back to Edinburgh to live with Andy, and we went busking with the Ugandan xylophone to earn money, as I had no job for a while. In summer it was great, as we earned about £20 a day due to all the tourists in Edinburgh. This meant we could live comfortably. In May, there was Beltane Fire Festival, a brilliant Pagan festival where a woman dressed as the May Queen would dance around the hill at the end of Princes Street, with several semi-naked, colourful painted devils dancing at her side. All the elements were represented, including fire, water, and wind, and people got very drunk. My friend Clarissa came up to celebrate with me and Andy, and we played the Ugandan amadinda xylophone to the crowd's delight.

Sometime later Andy's dad, Peter, announced: 'The Embaire group has been invited to perform at the Queen's Jubilee Celebrations'.

'That's brilliant, Dad' replied Andy, obviously really pleased about the news. 'We will get together a fabulous group of musicians'.

'It would be fantastic to have dancers as well', I exclaimed excitedly.

'Where will it take place?' Andy questioned.

'I understand it will be at Westminster Abbey', responded Peter, smiling at the joy his news had created.

During the following months, we had rehearsals at the School of Music at the University of Birmingham, where Andy's dad worked. Then we had rehearsals in London. The wonderful day came, which was an amazing event. We played right in front of the Queen and a huge audience. We had managed to get a troupe of great dancers, who performed wonderfully, gyrating their hips to the wild Ugandan sounds, and moving through the Abbey, as the audience screamed with glee.

**Peter practising embaire for the performance in
Westminster Abbey**

**Practising embaire for the Westminster Abbey performance (I am on
the far right)**

After leaving my employment in Dundee, I secured a job at a high-security hospital in Liverpool. I had previously read in the *Guardian* that there had been a public enquiry in 1992. The report said that patients had alleged sexual and physical abuse by staff, including women and men patients with learning disabilities, and it was reported that they wished to improve service for women patients. This had motivated me to apply for the job, and I decided to try my best to help.

Andy seemed upset about this, and we started having problems communicating. I found it very upsetting as I did not want to split up but had a feeling Andy did. I can recall feeling very distressed during this time and felt as though I could not see the point of life without him. He was my best friend as well as my partner. I never acted on these feelings, but it was a very tough time. We decided to give it a go and I moved to Liverpool. This was heart-wrenching for me, as I loved Andy and Edinburgh, but I needed to work. So, I moved, a decision I was later to regret.

Seven

Amadinda and Embaire – Wild Xylophones of Uganda

Andy suddenly announced: 'My dad is going to Uganda to record music; would you like to join us?' Andy's dad, Peter, was a Senior Lecturer in Ethnomusicology at Edinburgh University, and he studied Ugandan traditional music as part of his role.

I very excitedly agreed. I had never been to Africa before, so this was a dream come true. I spent the next couple of months feeling extremely excited and planning for our big adventure. Then the fabulous day finally came.

We flew to Kenya and drove straight through one of the game parks after landing in Nairobi. I remember thinking how big the sky seemed. In the UK, the sky seemed exceedingly small in comparison. I had a fantastic sense of space for the first time in my life and loved it; I felt I could really breathe and enjoyed the sounds, colours, people, birds, and wildlife. When we arrived in the game park, the beautiful morning sun was rising over the vast expanse of plains. I could hear colourful birds happily chirping, as if to greet us. I fell in love with the sounds, the vast feeling of space, and the beauty all around. I found the African trees wild and exciting, and I loved the interesting shapes. The mountains in the distance were a fabulous backdrop. The air somehow felt cleaner.

Andy, Peter, and I stayed with his friends in Nairobi in a beautiful house. It was a detached, converted farmhouse with several rooms and a huge garden. There was a music room full of traditional instruments from all over the world, as Peter's friend was also an academic musician. The garden was adorned with pretty flowers and blossoms, including one of my favourite jacaranda trees, which was full of bright purple radiance. After a few days of enjoying Kenya, we borrowed Peter's friend's Land Rover, which I discovered was the same one used in the film *Out of Africa*. I loved this film, and I had always had a thing for Robert Redford. I felt honoured to be travelling in a vehicle that appeared in his film.

We set off excitedly on our drive across Kenya to Uganda. We passed through the Rift Valley, which was stunningly beautiful, and stopped to walk around. It was great to see the mountains surrounding us, the valleys, and the huge sky. We then took a break at Lake Naivasha to see the pink flamingos. I love birds, and it was fantastic being able to see the swarms of pink flamingos enjoying themselves by the lake. It was fabulous to hear their squawks and see them flying around, having fun in the open air.

When we set off the following day to Uganda, I noticed that the Land Rover was making peculiar noises, but when I asked Peter, he dismissed it as 'nothing important'. After security checks at the border, we continued to Mbale in the east of Uganda. I was struck by its beauty, with green rolling hills and striking reddish brown soil shining in the African sun. It was so beautiful and colourful, and everyone was smiling. The clothes people wore were bright and bold, and there was a vivid and vibrant atmosphere, especially when we reached 'crazy Kampala', the capital city.

We stayed with the Kizza family – a family that Peter knew from when he had previously lived in Uganda. They made us feel very welcome, and from that moment we spent our time sharing stories and laughing. The Kizza family was huge; there was Nnalongo, their mother, whose name means 'mother of twins'; and the dad was Ssalongo, meaning 'father of twins'. Then there were the children: Charles, Peter, Paul, Christine, and Topher. There was also Kato and Wasswa, the twins. I thought I had found my family at last, as I fitted in so well and felt at home.

Left to right: Me, Peter, Andy and Nnalongo, having a meal at the Kizza family home

When we arrived in Kampala, our Land Rover completely broke down. Peter and Topher tried their best to fix it, then Kato – who was a young boy at the time – came to the rescue and repaired it. I was amazed at his skill at such a youthful age. I later taught him to swim at Silver Springs Hotel, after an incident where he had to be rescued after jumping in the deep end when he did not know how to swim. One of the lifeguards dived in and rescued him before I could plunge in myself. I felt an enormous sense of relief at what could have been a disaster. I was so scared by the incident that I started teaching him from that day forward. I am immensely proud to say that he is now a very talented swimmer.

I became close friends with the eldest son, Charles, and on my first visit to Kampala we visited its infamous taxi park. So many Ugandans asked me if I had been there, and I could sense why, as I have never seen so many small vehicles in such a tight space. I was amazed by how they expertly navigated their way in and out of the park, even though there seemed to be no space to do so. I was impressed by the amount of *matatus* (small people-carriers crammed with chickens and all kinds of belongings) huddled together, and so I took a photo.

Out of nowhere, a police officer appeared and followed us both into the *matatu* as we boarded to return home. He started shouting at me. I tried my best to ignore him. Charles looked very embarrassed and turned to me to say, *He wants a bribe, as he says you should not have taken the photo. Just ignore him.* I did. Then the irate police officer started demanding Charles' identity card. I got worried, as he was threatening to take Charles to prison. I had very sadly learnt the previous day that Charles was HIV positive, and I certainly did not wish to see him dragged off to prison in his condition. I therefore paid the bribe reluctantly and Charles was very humiliated, as we both knew that it was wrong. He sat angrily in the taxi back to our house, while I tried to assure him, we had done the best thing.

Andy and Peter were to visit musicians in Kampala the following day, so I decided to look around Kampala. I loved the chaos of Kampala, the liveliness of the streets, the colourful clothes, and the music blasting from every street corner. Everyone was friendly and more than happy to chat, interested to hear why the Mzungu had come to visit Uganda. I was made to feel very welcome, loved, and special. I viewed a beautiful cathedral on a hill and decided to walk up and look around. I entered the beautiful building and after several minutes a nun approached me. She explained that this was Namirembe Cathedral. The nun showed me around and then we went outside to admire the views all over Kampala.

'What is your name?' the nun suddenly asked.

'Helen', I said.

'Well, in Uganda, you will be given the name Nalule', she said.

I was honoured to be given a Ugandan name. 'What does it mean?' I asked.

'It means bringer of good things', responded the nun.

'That's lovely'. I was pleased with the name, but also a bit concerned regarding the meaning and the expectations that may arise from it.

'Nalule belongs to the Nyonge Clan. They are the otters', explained the nun.

'That's very fitting', I said, 'as I love swimming'.

I had a brilliant feeling of being understood, and although I had not mentioned my love of swimming, the nun seemed to know me already. I returned to the Kizzas and excitedly told Andy the story. Later, we all sat down to eat and shared our stories of the day, and I felt a wonderful warm glow of belonging.

A few days later, we set off to Busoga, Eastern Uganda, to record traditional music. Who would have thought I would find myself wildly dancing and shaking my pelvis as fast as is humanely possible with Andy, to exciting xylophone music in a remote Ugandan village in 1992. The huge

Peter (far right) and Seby (at left) playing embaire (xylophone)

62

crowd that had gathered screamed and shouted happily as they watched the *Bazungu* (white people) engaging in Busoga dance. The hot sun shone brightly on the beautiful rich red soil, and we were surrounded by bright clothes, huge smiles, laughter, and wild greenery. I noticed that Peter was desperately trying to get his recording gear set up quickly. He assembled the microphone in a tree over the instrument near the main vocalist just before the musicians started playing. He looked relieved about not missing any of the amazing musical feast.

We travelled to Nakibembe Xylophone Group where Ugandan musicians and dancers warmly welcomed us. It took several hours of chatting to our excited crowd before the musicians had dug a huge pit in the ground. I wondered what they were doing. I then saw them laying down the 21-key-embaire on two banana stems while vast crowds gathered in amazement and wonder at the only *Bazungu* for miles. I felt very at home; the atmosphere was electric. I ordered a 15-key xylophone to be made and was informed by a xylophone maker that I would also need to pay for a chicken. I tried to ask why but was told it would be a surprise. We all returned to Kampala, with me questioning why I had left money for a chicken.

Sometime later, I received a message that my wooden xylophone was ready to be collected. We all drove back to Busoga and left the vehicle in Iganga, the nearest small town to Nakibembe. We boarded a *matatu* and then rode on the back of *boda boda* (motorbikes) with all our recording equipment. I had fallen in love with Uganda, the friendly hospitable people, the beauty of the country, the rolling green hills and glorious red sand, and the wealth of colour.

As we entered the wooded rural area, each of us riding a small motorbike, a sense of foreboding crept up on me. *Goodness, we could be kidnapped*

Me (left) and Mugwisa (right) playing the *endongo* (thumb piano)

or murdered, and no-one would ever know, I thought to myself. Uganda's history with the atrocities conducted by Amin and others was etched in my mind, but this trip was to open my mind. As we got closer, I spotted my 15-key wooden xylophone very beautifully painted on every note. All my morbid thoughts immediately left my head and were replaced with excited enthusiasm when I saw the beautiful workmanship that had produced my delightful new instrument.

I was asked by Mugwisa, the xylophone maker, to go into the banana plantations, where I was met by the leaders of the group as well as a live chicken – squawking aggressively as if it knew something was about to happen. One of the musicians held the chicken and suddenly cut its throat. Blood spurted everywhere. *Oh, I do not much like this*, I thought, being a vegetarian. The musicians poured the remaining blood on the middle key of the xylophone.

'Why do you do this?' I asked quizzically, and Mugwisa replied. 'Whenever we make a xylophone, we pay our respects to the elders who started the xylophone-making tradition in this village. We pour blood on the middle key to give the xylophone its heart, otherwise it will not sound good'.

'Oh, I see', I said, feeling very privileged to learn the history of this musical tradition in Busoga. 'What do you kill if I buy a twenty-one key embaire?'

Mugwisa laughed. 'A goat', he replied with a smile. I also smirked, although I did not approve of an animal being slaughtered.

The wild music continued to celebrate the christening of my xylophone with eight energetic musicians. They sat over the instrument whilst frantically beating an octave with a stick in each hand, four musicians on one side and four on the other. The most amazing sound emerged from the interlocking tunes. The largest twenty-one key was so big that the musicians also used it as a drum, beating the centre with their hand whilst playing the xylophone at the same time. The embaire players were joined by other musicians shaking *nsassi* (shakers), and *endingidi* (tube fiddles) – a small African violin with one string – and a flute player.

The crowd got bigger and bigger, with people coming from all the surrounding villages. Screaming pierced the air as two male Ugandan dancers suddenly appeared wildly wiggling their hips and pelvises as fast as humanly possible. It was very sexy, energetic dancing. On occasion, they would move remarkably close to unsuspecting women in the crowd, who would look very embarrassed and then hand the dancers Ugandan schillings. Andy, Peter, and I became red in the face when the gyrating male dancers 'shook their jigs' in front of us. We all laughed in embarrassment and gave money, then joined in with the energetic hip wiggling much to the hilarity and screaming of the gathered crowd.

After a couple of very enjoyable hours, the performance reached its climax and ended when it had become dark. We made our way back to Iganga, where we stayed for the night in a dubious hotel. We stopped for lunch on the way home and listened to our recordings. We were all still feeling extremely excited and elated by the beautiful sounds, lively audience, musicians, bright colours, my embaire xylophone, and of course the mysterious chicken.

To get to the hotel, we had to walk past a barber, where men were sitting having their hair done. They would happily greet you as you walked above them. There were a few rooms directly above. The man who showed us round had limited English and amused us by saying, 'Isn't it?' in response to everything we asked him. Next morning, Andy pointed out what we thought were bed bug bites all over his neck. We moved hotels, but the following night I was disturbed by something large and slippery crawling about in my hair. I leapt out of my bed when I realised it was a cockroach. Suddenly the original hotel did not seem so bad. We went back, and Mr 'isn't it?' assured us that he had dealt with the bed bugs. At a discounted rate, we agreed to return.

During our stay in Busoga, we visited Nile Beat Artists in Jinja and recorded their performance at the source of the Nile by Lake Victoria. It was a beautiful setting and very peaceful. We had a lovely boat ride and saw beautiful birds, including grey herons, egrets, fish eagles, and others. I bought an *endongo* from Walusimbe, one of the musicians in Nile Beat Artists. I loved the simplicity of the thumb piano, which was a wooden box with a hole in it and beaten-down bicycle spokes lying across it. You plucked these with your thumb, and it made a fantastic sound. Sometimes I would go to the local market to have false nails put on my thumbs to play better. This caused great hilarity to the Ugandans, who wondered why I was not having all my nails done. I also met Seby, one of the musicians in the group, who I got on very well with. I had thumb piano lessons and made great recordings.

We returned to Kampala incredibly happy and recorded other musicians during our holiday. We met the now late Albert Ssempeke, a traditional musician from Kampala, who sang beautifully and played traditional instruments including the lyre, a Ugandan harp. He took us to his small house, which was quite simple, with only a bed and a radio. I could not believe it when he told me he had thirty children and six wives. I wondered how he could afford them all. He was especially kind to me, and we spent many hours talking and learning xylophone together. Ssempeke took Andy and me to the drum-makers, as Andy was buying instruments to take back to the UK. He then took us both to the Kabaka's Lake. He showed us the part of the lake dedicated to our bestowed clans. Mine (Nalule) was Nnyonyi, the otter clan, and Andy's (Mukasa Ssali) belonged to the Nkima monkey clan. Andy also introduced me to Bernard Kabanda and Bakka, two other traditional musicians who lived in Kawempe. Bernard played Kadongo Kamu, which means 'my little guitar'. He had a guitar which he had made himself out of wood, with stickers of various places he had visited.

The trip to Uganda changed my life, and I was so sad when we had to leave. A few days before we left, I went to Makerere University, the main university in Kampala, and visited the Psychology Department. They were pleased to see me and asked me if I could assist them in starting a master's course in clinical psychology. I met psychology lecturers there, including Rebecca. Rebecca and I became very friendly and discussed the possibilities of starting the clinical psychology course. When I returned to the UK, I applied for the British Psychological Society Visiting Psychologist Scheme. This would bring Rebecca to the UK to visit Liverpool and Manchester universities, as well as to the British Council to see if we could establish links and start the clinical psychology programme.

Eight

Adventures in the South African Sea and Nepalese Mountains

Andy came to visit while I was living in Liverpool, and I also travelled to Edinburgh to see him, but this was a difficult period. Although I still loved him, I ended the relationship and told him I did not want to see him for at least six months. I took him to the train station in Liverpool and can clearly recall him saying that he still loved me as he got on the train. It really broke my heart, and I do not know to this day how I managed to recover from it. I walked about in a daze for several months, wondering what I had done. I think focussing on my new job, making new friends in Liverpool, and exploring the city helped me. It was a life-changing event that really broke my heart, but at the same time provided the opportunity to continue my links with and love of Africa. My life could have been vastly different if I had not met Andy and visited Uganda, and this is something I would always be grateful for.

After a year or so of Andy and I separating, I met Neil in Liverpool. Neil was a friendly and very funny Irish man, and he was splitting up with his partner. We used to have fun going to gay clubs and seeing bands. He was having a stressful time ending his relationship. After it ended, Neil had already decided to take a year off and travel around the world. I took the opportunity to meet him in various places.

On the first trip, I met him in Nepal, and we walked the Annapurna Circuit, which was meant to take over fourteen days. However, Neil wanted to do it in eleven. When we met in Pokhara, I found he had changed his name from Neil to Leo, in the hope it would bring him better luck. He was going through a challenging time, as was I, but the trip was fabulous and the views and people in Nepal were magnificent. They were friendly and humble. This was different to the UK, where people kept themselves isolated in their own houses, preferring their own space. The Nepalese seemed calm and adapted to their surroundings. I was also impressed by the vast volumes of luggage they carried without seeming to notice the heavy weights. I loved the bustle of Pokhara, with lively cafés and bars surrounded by beautiful mountains. We went out for meals and spent time organising our walking trip. I was amused by the cows walking around the streets, which would approach you whilst you were eating in restaurants, as if they wanted to join you for the meal.

We set off on our adventure in Annapurna. Despite hurting my ankle and wanting to rest, Leo was anxious to keep walking, and we did complete the walk in eleven days. Luckily, my ankle recovered quickly, and we continued navigating the beautiful surroundings. The scenery was gorgeous, populated by colourful rhododendron flowers and stunning mountains. The walking was very tough and involved climbing up never-ending stairs. I found myself counting the number of steps to help me get up the steep slopes. We stayed overnight in small lodges, and I soon developed a liking for meals made with Yak's cheese, including pizza. I enjoyed talking with the Nepalese guides while we sat around eating. I was worried about mountain sickness, as I was not very fit. One evening I asked our Nepalese guide how I could avoid it.

'Well, I know the West recommends tablets, but we don't think they are helpful', replied the Nepalese guide.

'What do you recommend?' I enquired.

'Eating garlic', came the reply.

'How does eating garlic help?'

'It thins the blood and enables you to breathe more easily'.

Having seen walkers lying on the paths or having to give up their trek due to altitude sickness, I was determined to do my best not to get it. I had something with garlic every night and ate copious amounts of garlic soup, garlic pizza, and garlic bread. Leo also joined in. I had a bit of altitude sickness, but when we descended another hundred metres it went away. This led me to be convinced that the Nepalese were incredibly wise with their local cultural advice.

When we reached base camp, there was fresh snow and stunning blue skies. We saw a Russian team climbing the big, beautiful mountain that the Nepalese called the 'fishtail', in the north-central region of Nepal. Its real name is Machapuchare; it was named this by the Nepalese as from a distance, its shape looks like an upside-down fish tail. I met two gay men who were very friendly, and we spent the evenings chatting and laughing with them.

On the way back down, we were welcomed by some hot springs in the mountains. We quickly got into our swimming costumes and dipped our aching limbs in the water. It was beautiful and relaxing, and my sore muscles certainly appreciated it. However, the smell of sulphur was a bit off-putting. I consoled myself by breathing through my mouth and focussing on the beautiful scenery around us, with mountains covered in snow and stunningly attractive flowers.

We spent the last day before I flew back to the UK in Kathmandu and said goodbye at the airport. When I arrived at passport control, I suddenly felt extremely ill. I had to run to the toilets, where I vomited disgusting black stuff and felt very poorly with a fever. I do not know how I managed the flight to Delhi, where I had a twelve-hour stopover that I spent trying to recover in my hotel.

Some months later, Leo invited me to meet him in Cape Town, where we went scuba diving and enjoyed exploring the sights. The lure of travelling

White water rafting on the Zambezi River

to a country I had never been to before made it exciting. I have returned several times since this initial visit and have become an associate researcher at the Gender, Health, and Justice Research Centre at the University of Cape Town, although I am still based in the UK. I loved Cape Town; the dramatic coastline and the huge mountains surrounding the sea. I was disappointed that we only had a few days there. We then flew to Zimbabwe. I was a little hesitant about the trip, but the lure of travelling to countries I had never been to before decided it for me.

We had a great adventure in Zimbabwe. We stayed with Leo's relatives in Bulawayo and went out on the anniversary of Independence Day when Rhodesia became Zimbabwe. This was not the most sensible idea, as we tried to go to a music celebration and our taxi had rocks hurled towards it, so we left promptly. We returned to the safety of Leo's relatives' house, which was well-guarded and fenced up to the hilt. Soon afterwards, we took the overnight train and celebrated the new year on the way to Victoria Falls.

When we reached Victoria Falls, we decided to try white water rafting. During our first adventure and each time we fell out of the boat, it felt like I was going to drown. I was practically cartwheeling into the water, as though we were being spun around in a washing machine with no hope of ever reaching the surface for air. There were also crocodiles in the river, and when I finally reached the surface to take a breath, I saw that none of my other boat friends could be seen, or the boat for that matter.

Back row left to right: Leo (left hand side, third from the front) and Me (right hand side, second from the front), white water rafting on the Zambezi River

A person on a kayak came up and asked if I was okay. I answered, 'No, not really', after swallowing what seemed like half of the Zambezi River. They pulled me back to the boat, where I was lifted back in only for the boat to capsize again at the next rapids. I do not know how we survived the day, as I was sure I was going to die, but we did. We later discovered that two boat-loads of people had been killed two weeks previously, which did not surprise me. After we had endured the day's excitement, a photographer approached enthusiastically, saying: 'Look at this, isn't it brilliant?'

I cast my eyes down to the photograph he was showing me and saw that it was an amazing picture of our boat getting catapulted far into the air at a ninety-degree angle to the water below. I saw that all of us were captured in mid-air falling backwards out of the boat, suspended above the water. I thanked him very much for the picture and understood why I had thought I was on the verge of death.

The second adventure we had was swimming on top of Victoria Falls. We had crossed the border and walked into Zambia. There was a ledge with a small pool into which you could just about squeeze. I had to cling onto the rocks to make sure I did not fall over the edge, which I doubted anyone would survive. I have photos of Leo balancing right on the edge of the one-hundred-metre drop (see below). It was very scary, but exhilarating. On reflection, Leo stated he would not do this again, but it was a lot of fun at the time.

Left to right: Swimming in Devil's Pool, Zambia

Left to right: Pilot and Me, about to fly a microlight in Zambia

On the third adventure, we went up in a double microlight, which was amazing. We took it in turns flying all over the falls. The pilot suddenly swooped down over the river, so that we could see all the hippos. There was just a strap holding me in, and the rest of the microlight was open to the air. The experience was beautiful and very exhilarating.

It was a superb trip and we have stayed brilliant friends, and still have fun together when we meet. Leo returned to Ireland after his year around the world and later married an Irish woman. They now have three children, a dog, a cat, and two goats.

Nine

Supporting Survivors—and Musical Adventures in Uganda

Soon after returning from Uganda in 1992, I learned I had secured a job as a Senior Clinical Psychologist at a high-security hospital, and so I moved to Liverpool. Initially, I lived at the hospital in a shared flat. It was several miles from Liverpool. The accommodation felt 'cut off' from normal life. I settled into my post and enjoyed it, although I was a bit disappointed initially about having to work on the male wards as well as the female wards. I had moved there specifically to work with women following the public inquiry into the abuse of women patients and male patients with learning disabilities at the hospital (*Report of the Committee of Inquiry into the Personality Disorder Unit, 1999; 2002*).

I had two supervisors, who were both friendly and supportive of my work, for which I was grateful. Due to my previous experiences, this was not expected. I provided therapy for several patients, including a male patient who had committed murder but did well in individual therapy. He asked if I would take him on a day out to the Liverpool city centre. After discussing it with the team, it was decided we could go with his key nurse. Unfortunately, whilst we were out shopping, he tried to ask me out, and started telling me he loved me. I knew this to be what psychologists call 'transference', which had to happen for therapy to be successful. However, I realised this a bit too late while the patient was declaring his love for me in the middle of Marks and Spencer. I realised that this had been a bad idea.

Although I tried my best to placate the situation, he became incredibly angry and smashed the front doors of the store. After what seemed like forever, the transport arrived to take us back to the hospital. This event did not go down well with the care team, who tried to stop his therapy sessions with me. However, through sensitive negotiation, I did continue to see him under supervision, and he progressed well. We were able to deal with the transference issues of his 'love' for me, and he accepted that this was part of the process of therapy and became more realistic about the relationship.

After about six months of working at the hospital, I was relocated full-time to work with women and became the lead for women's services. I had only been qualified for two years at this point. However, I took the post full of optimism and managed to get two trainee clinical psychologists and an assistant psychologist to work with me. We conducted a four-year research programme and interviewed women patients about why they self-harmed, as well as staff regarding their experiences (*Liebling & Chipchase, 1993, 1995, 2000; Chipchase & Liebling, 1996; Liebling, Chipchase & Velangi, 1997*). I also set up a therapy group for women who self-harmed and evaluated this for my master's degree in forensic behavioural science, which I studied at Liverpool University. I was able to complete my master's degree part-time whilst also working at the high-security hospital.

As I felt isolated at the hospital, I decided to move into a shared house, which was a co-operative, and soon became friends with Claire. We shared similar views and were both feminist in our thinking.

Left to right: Ruth, Me, and Claire on holiday in Dorset

Raymond and I started going out about one year after Leo and I had split up. We initially got on well and had the same interests. He was a social worker, so understood my work. We also shared a love of music and art. After some months, I had to move out of my accommodation, so we moved in together. This did not work out quite as I had expected. Problems started with a small incident, which at first did not mean anything, but gradually I suspected he may have been drinking. He would sometimes refuse to let me back in his house if I went out with friends – and got jealous. After a few weeks, I moved out and got my own flat. However, his behaviour became more worrying. On one occasion, he did not wish for me to travel for a weekend away with friends. I ended the relationship but felt worried about what he might do. My friends helped me to move to Bradford.

Unfortunately, the more I tried to work with women therapeutically, the more I became aware that the abuses I had read about in the public inquiry report (*Blom-Cooper et al. 1992*) were still happening. We set up a therapy group and were told off by the hospital staff for bringing in pizza when it was one of the patient's birthdays. It seemed that anything kind or therapeutic we did would just land us in trouble. The staff at the hospital tried to stop the women's group from meeting, but we managed to keep it going by sheer grit and determination, and the women patients told us they very much valued it.

Women patients complained frequently about their poor treatment by staff and sometimes male patients, which included allegations of psychological, physical, and sexual abuse. One of the psychiatrists at the time appeared to fear women and operated very punitive treatments, which led to increased levels of self-harm and suicidal behaviours. He appeared at times not to follow professional protocols and changed women's diagnoses and their medication. I recall him telling me once that his wife had the best job: 'She is a pathologist, so does not have to speak to patients, just cuts them up.'

I replied, 'Why on earth did you become a psychiatrist?' He did not reply and just shrugged his shoulders, demonstrating a lack of insight. This concerned me.

The more I supported women at the hospital, the more difficult my role became. Several women my colleagues and I worked with made allegations of abuse by staff. This placed me in an extremely uncomfortable situation, where I was raising their complaints at the hospital to no avail. I then involved Women in Special Hospitals and the Mental Health Act Commission to raise their concerns externally. Things were getting increasingly difficult, and I also became concerned for my own safety due to the incidents I was exposing. I was extremely aware that whistle-blowers in the 1992 inquiry had been targeted by staff at the hospital.

In June 1985, a patient complained to me that she had been sexually assaulted by a male nurse and showed me the bruises on her thighs. Despite repeated attempts to get the allegations taken seriously and to involve the police and the Mental Health Act Commission, no action was taken by either the hospital, the Mental Health Act Commission, or the police. I also objected to one of the women having ECT (Electroconvulsive Therapy), which in my view was an unwarranted attempt to silence and control her. Shortly after expressing my concerns at a care team meeting regarding these incidents, I was suspended from my post.

Despite this terrible situation in the women's group and with my women colleagues, we were often able to laugh about the situation, even though what was happening was profoundly serious. In the women's therapy group, there was humour, although the women also shared very painful memories and experiences. I became acutely aware of the power that women held to survive exceedingly tricky situations.

A colleague told me later that another psychiatrist had laughed in front of the team about the fact that I was suspended. At this point, my colleague spoke up and told him that I was walking past the window. She related that he went pale and looked like he was about to faint. I later returned to work, as it turned out the hospital could not suspend me for having a difference of opinion.

I realised shortly after this that my position was becoming untenable, so I made the decision to resign from my post and claim constructive dismissal and sexual discrimination. Other colleagues had taken this action previously after speaking out. It was to me the best and most ethical option. Young women who I supervised alleged that a staff member was harassing them, and I did not want to end up in the same position. One of my supervisors, who shared the same concerns, also left the high-security hospital, and offered me a job in Leeds, which I took. Although I wished to move, I still found the change tricky, as I was settled in Liverpool with friends and did not know anyone in Bradford.

The job in Yorkshire went well. We were a team of five professionals conducting court reports for compensation cases. Our focus was adult men who had been sexually, physically, and psychologically abused in care homes in the north-west of the United Kingdom. The abuse was on a horrific scale, with hundreds of boys having survived abuse. My role was to interview the men, who were often in prison because of their experiences, and to draft a report for the solicitors. The legal firm would then take what they termed a lead case of one boy in the home to court, and if that case won, all the men who had been abused in the same home would receive compensation. I found the work remarkably interesting and liked the fact that we were trying our best with the solicitors to get justice for the men's experiences. When the cases went to court several years afterwards, all the men I had authored reports for were successful in their claims. The fact they got justice for their suffering made me incredibly happy. The men also told me that they felt our belief in them would aid their recovery.

As well as doing the court work, I worked in Yorkshire in adult mental health services and in a psychiatric hospital on the women's secure ward. It was good to be with two colleagues who had worked in secure hospitals.

They were incredibly supportive of my industrial tribunal. It was a tough time, as there were meetings with solicitors about the court case. The high-security hospital did their best to try to knock out the sexual harassment claim, which I resisted. During this period, there was tremendous pressure on me. However, my determination to fight for justice and the rights of women survivors at the hospital motivated me to continue.

After I had been working in Yorkshire for a few months, I learnt that one of the women patients I had tried my best to get out of the hospital had died there. I was very distressed about the incident, and subsequently found out that her body was cremated. I then knew that any evidence related to the circumstances of her death could no longer be proven. I had several documents relating to her situation, which I submitted as evidence in my tribunal. Her death upset me to the very core and did not resolve anything for me regarding the abuses prevalent at the hospital. All the wrongdoings were silenced, and it was incredibly sad. In the end, the hospital asked me to agree to a silencing clause, which I would not do. I was strongly advised by my solicitor to take a cash payment and their admission of guilt without a silencing clause, which I did. I was disappointed not to have my time in court, but the press publicised the fact that I had won my case. On reflection, I am extremely pleased by how well I did.

Soon afterwards, there was an allegation that a young girl had been taken to the hospital and was subsequently abused by sex offenders. The Fallon Inquiry (*Report of the Committee of Inquiry into the Personality Disorder Unit, Ashworth Special Hospital, 1999*) into the Hospital events was initiated. I took the opportunity to submit all my evidence from the industrial tribunal to the Fallon inquiry, including the evidence regarding the woman who had died, in the hope that they would extend their remit to look at the abuse of women patients.

The inquest gave a verdict of accidental death, but I was never convinced, and to this day am suspicious. She was a very outspoken woman who was targeted by staff in several ways, as well as given ECT against her will. I had found her crying in her room following ECT. She explained that two psychiatrists insisted she sign the consent form to have ECT, otherwise they would stop her from seeing her boyfriend, a male patient at the hospital and the only support she had. I was appalled. I was very distressed and traumatised by her death, as in my view she should have been out of the hospital and safe. I had been trying extremely hard to ensure this happened.

I was pleased by the tribunal result and felt vindicated. Then the Fallon Inquiry (*Report of the Committee of Inquiry into the Personality Disorder Unit, Ashworth Special Hospital, 1999*) concluded that there was a 'culture of sexual exploitation' at the hospital, which further supported my experiences of the lack of moral care. It further recommended that all the women patients be moved to other hospitals. That was a great achievement, and I knew then that although the woman had died, she had at least not died in vain.

A woman clinical psychologist, and a strong advocate for service users, interviewed those of us working with women patients about our experiences (*Liebling et al, 1998*). However, the whole experience of fighting for what was morally right left me feeling completely disillusioned about mental health services in the UK. At around the same time the Yorkshire NHS Trust closed our service, as it was the view of some of the managers that we had not generated enough income. There appeared to be a misunderstanding regarding how the service had been set up, and one of our team members launched an industrial tribunal against the health authority. We were all made redundant, but at the same time I was offered a post as a senior lecturer at a University in Kampala, Uganda.

I helped the university start the clinical psychology course we had spoken about, and although the post was on local wages, I thought the experience would be invaluable. I took the post, packed my bags and teaching materials, and went to the airport to fly to Entebbe. I started my new job in Kampala in September 1987.

Ten

'Bernard' – A Chicken on the Bus

Whilst I was still working at the high-security hospital, Andy had organised a tour with WOMAD, World of Music Arts and Dance, for Bernard Kabanda and Bakkabulindi Samuel, two traditional musicians based in Kawepeke, Kampala.

I was introduced to Bernard by Andy while I was working at a university in Kampala. He would arrive at my small university shared house to play *kadongo kamu* (my little guitar), carrying his old rustic guitar made from spare parts. He had built the instrument himself and it contained stickers of the places in the world he had performed at. We busked together in Wandergere, a lively drinking hole populated by Ugandans who wished to have an enjoyable time. Bernard would shout out, 'Lukumi for a song!' Then someone in the audience would excitedly throw the money, and Bernard would whack out very wild beats on his guitar whilst strutting his stuff to the delight of the audience. At the same time, I would shake *enseege* (a shaker full of seeds), as well as my *booty* (behind), performing traditional Ugandan dancing. This seemed to come naturally to me and caused hilarity amongst the Ugandan audience. Sometimes men, women, and children would join us in wild dancing too, to show me how it should really be done.

I recall being with Andy at the Ugandan museum when Bernard strutted into one of Albert Ssempeke's rehearsals and proudly pulled out a suitcase. He announced to his friends, 'I'm going on a tour of the world with WOMAD'. I went to see them perform and was so proud to see my friends from Uganda performing as part of a WOMAD tour. Peter Gabriel invited them to record a CD in his studios while they were in the UK. Sadly, towards the end of their WOMAD tour, Bernard became extremely ill. He was HIV positive. He unfortunately died three weeks later while they were performing in the USA. WOMAD kindly flew his body back to Uganda. In Bernard's inimitable style, he had managed to enjoy all his earnings and partied his last days away.

Sometime later, we arrived at Bernard's mother's small mud-hut, with its four small rooms: a kitchen, lounge, bathroom, and bedroom. Banana plants grew majestically in the garden where the late Bernard Kabanda was now buried. We had travelled to Kiboga District to pay our respects at Bernard's grave. As I stood mourning my friend's death, I was acutely aware that this revealed for me the stark contrast between the death of a patient at the high-security hospital and the death of a talented musician. The patients had died through lack of moral care by those who were commissioned to look after them, while Bernard, an incredibly talented musician, had died of AIDS after living a happy, free, and vibrant life.

It also brought home the helplessness I had felt in trying so hard to save the woman. She was not guilty of any crime but protecting her sister from severe abuse and had ended up in prison. She had been transferred to the hospital for her own safety, as she was suicidal, not dangerous. It all felt so unfair, and both their deaths touched my heart very much. Bernard's mother, who was poor, now had Bernard's four children to care for. She took this in her stride.

I first met 'Bernard the chicken' when he came squawking and flapping into my arms from Bernard's mother. He was a present, despite her being so poor. This really touched me. As Bernard the chicken lay in my arms, I did not have the heart to tell Bernard's mother that I was a vegetarian and did not, in fact, eat chicken. Bakka and I named the chicken on the bus on our way back from his mother's house:

'What shall we call him?' I asked, while sitting with the chicken on my lap.

'Let's call him Bernard, in honour of our friend who died', responded Bakka.

The *matatu* was made even livelier by me, Bakka, and Bernard strutting down the bus. The chicken chattered between us on the back seat, much to the amusement of the other passengers. They seemed amazed to see a *mzungu* (white person) carrying a chicken all the way to Kampala. Bernard got up to all kinds of exploits, flapping about, jumping under the seats, nibbling people's toes, and squawking at the top of his voice. This reminded me of the human Bernard's excitement when Peter Gabriel had asked him and Bakka to record a CD at his studios. Their song *Olugendo Lw'e Bulaya (The Journey to Europe)* was played during the film *Hotel Rwanda* and can still be found online today. I had been glad to see Bernard's mother's face light up when I had handed over the hard-earned money from the CD sales, and Bernard (the chicken) jumped about as if to acknowledge her joyousness and relief that it had been too late for Bernard to spend it all. I noticed Bernard's hopping around the bus and the movements were rhythmically in beat. Just like the real Bernard, who would strut his stuff to the delight of huge audiences.

After six bumpy, fun-filled hours, all of us were covered in dust. Bakka started to get off the bus, as we had arrived in 'crazy' Kampala Bus Park, so I hastily said, 'Hey, Bakka, you'd better take Bernard since I'm a vegetarian'. Bakka smiled, as did the others on the bus, and mumbled: 'Muzungu Nalule kwogera Luganda', meaning 'the white woman called Nalule speaks Ugandan'.

Every time I saw Bakka afterwards, I would ask after our friend Bernard, and he would remark; 'Bernard's getting fat'; 'Bernard's getting fatter'; 'Bernard's really fat now'. I smiled to myself, as Bernard had been so thin in real life. I considered it ironic as fatness in Uganda was considered a sign of health and wealth. Then one day, I asked Bakka, 'Have you eaten Bernard yet?'

He replied, 'No, Nalule, I do not have the heart to eat our friend'.

Sometime later, I asked after Bernard, and Bakka smirked. 'You won't believe it', he said, 'Bernard escaped'.

I smiled to myself. *Well, there you go,* I thought. *Bernard got the last laugh by escaping being eaten so he could continue strutting his stuff like he always used to.*

Eleven

Women Survivors and the Power of Music

I arrived at the airport and was checking in when the woman at the counter asked to weigh my hand luggage. *Strange, they do not usually do this*, I thought to myself. Unfortunately, I had put all the heavy books and my computer in my hand luggage. She then announced I would need to pay £400, as my bags were over the weight limit.

'But I am going to work at a university in Uganda on local wages' I pleaded.

'Those are the rules. You need to pay the fee'.

'I am carrying books and a computer for the department where I will be working. They hardly have any resources for the students I will be teaching. Please, can you find another solution? I will only be earning about £100 a month', I said.

'You have to pay £400, or you won't be boarding the airplane', replied the woman.

I was truly angry, as she was very harsh and insistent. I paid the money reluctantly. When I got on the aeroplane, there were hardly any people on it. *Oh, that is why she insisted on charging me so much. To try and recoup the loss of not having many passengers.* I then felt even angrier about the injustice of it all.

I excitedly arrived in Uganda and then at the university, where I was initially accommodated in the guest house. I started work but missed seeing my friends from the UK, particularly Raymond. He posted me out a tape with some great songs on it, which I listened to a lot to keep from getting lonely. However, the love songs made me miss him even more. I started to wonder if I had made a mistake.

The head of department was an American woman, and I was sometimes upset by how she treated the Ugandan staff. However, I started my work, which was to help run the clinical psychology course and the master's course in Counselling. I quickly became friends with the Ugandan staff and saw the Kizza family regularly. I got on well with the vice chancellor, and he soon moved me into a shared house at the university with other students. We became friends, and at weekends I would often travel to Busoga, Eastern Uganda, to play music with my Ugandan musician friends. I loved doing this, as it created a brilliant peaceful change from crazy Kampala. The streets of Jinja town were quiet and I travelled around on the back of a bicycle, enjoying the beautiful colours, contrasting smells of burning charcoal and flowers, and the hot sun on my body. There were five students enrolled for the clinical psychology course, and I felt immensely proud to be a major part of setting up and starting the running of the first clinical psychology course in East Africa.

After being in Uganda for a few months in 1988, I had met Ruth Ojiambo-Ochieng from an international non-government organisation called Women's International Peace Centre (formerly Isis-WICCE, Women's International Cross-Cultural Exchange), based in Kampala. Women's International Peace Centre is a feminist organisation with a mission to ignite women's leadership, amplify their voices, and deepen their activism in re-creating peace. The centre started out in 1974 as a global resource centre for women human rights defenders to document and disseminate women's own experiences, concerns, and ideas for ending gender inequality. In 1994, they moved from Geneva to Uganda, carving out documentation about women, peace, and security. The centre uses its own WEAVE (Women's Education for Advancement and Empowerment) model to catalyse women's power for peace by integrating research, documentation, holistic healing, skills, and movement building, as well as advocacy. Women's International Peace Centre works with partners in conflict-affected settings and with regional institutions in Africa and Asia to ensure that women not only powerfully contribute to peace-building processes and results, but also transform these spaces to be more gender inclusive and gender responsive.

I warmed to Ruth immediately. She was an incredibly positive, passionate woman who put her heart and soul into the fight for gender equality and justice. She was a force to be reckoned with and we would become great colleagues and friends. Whilst I was working at the university, Ruth invited me to join a Ugandan team of health professionals who were conducting a medical and psychological intervention for women conflict survivors of sexual and gender-based violence (SGBV) in Luwero District. Luwero is about two hours' drive from Kampala. It is still an extremely poor area due to the terrible devastation of years of conflict, as well as viruses that had attacked the trees. I found it beautiful, with huge volumes of green banana trees, stunning red soil, and the best watermelons and pineapples I have ever eaten in my life. The staple diet of Uganda and Luwero is *matoke*, which is made from boiling green bananas in their leaves and then mashing them into a consistency like mashed potatoes. I did not enjoy *matoke*, but I loved the sight of a striking variety of green banana trees all around.

The dedicated staff of Women's International Peace Centre had previously spent two years in Luwero sensitising women and listening to their experiences of conflict to gain their trust. It was after this period, when trust had developed, that they started disclosing their experiences of SGBV, including the rapes they endured. Following this, they were also able to come forward for treatment to resolve their long-standing health problems. I was delighted and honoured to be invited to be the clinical psychologist in the Ugandan-led team for the project. At this point, there were no Ugandan clinical psychologists trained, so it was entirely appropriate to assist the team.

The funding for the intervention was obtained from Medica Mondiale, based in Germany. I travelled with a multidisciplinary team of Ugandan health workers to provide medical, psychological, and gynaecological services to two hundred and thirty-seven war-affected women in Luwero. This intervention was provided by a collaboration of WIPC and APRO (African Psycare Research Organisation), and it included psychiatrists, social workers, and psychologists, as well as members of the counselling services at Makerere University.

APRO is a Ugandan-based organisation whose main function is to conduct research and training and provide emotional health and well-being services, particularly to conflict-torture and SGBV survivors in Uganda. The Association of Obstetricians and Gynaecologists of Uganda (AGOU) provided screening and interventions.

We arrived at a health centre in Kikamulo Sub-County and set ourselves up in a few rooms. I noticed there was a long queue of women waiting, who greeted us enthusiastically when we arrived. The first part of the intervention involved screening forty-eight women conflict survivors over a period of three days. This screening involved an assessment of demographic information and women's experiences during the conflict, including the traumatic impact. The study found that women were tortured during the conflict, and 54.4% suffered sexual violence including rapes, being abducted as sex slaves, forced into marriages with abductors, and other violations. Of the women screened, 54.2% presented with post-traumatic stress, as well as physical and gynaecological health difficulties due to the serious impact of their experiences. Women also experienced physical aches and pains, headaches, genital and abdominal pains, palpitations, chest pains, anxiety, lack of appetite, and ulcers.

Interviewing the women was a very humbling experience. I collaborated closely with a trusted interpreter who translated word-for-word the women's Luganda into English. I was struck by the way the women confided in me, despite my being a stranger to them. Yet I knew that the women could see that the organisation was not only collecting their narratives, but truly trying to assist them with the ongoing impact of their experiences.

The second part of the intervention comprised a qualitative analysis of the psychological consequences of conflict in two hundred and thirty-seven women. This was collated using in-depth interviews of women's conflict-related experiences. The third part of the intervention identified gynaecological effects and provided treatment for those affected.

Our project concluded: 'The effects of the war on the women have impeded their daily functioning and impacted on the low socio-economic development of this region despite massive infrastructural and economic rehabilitation efforts by the government' (*Musisi et al, 1999: 4*). It further recommended that: 'a psycho-traumatic treatment programme be implemented as a matter of priority for these war survivors'.

Women's experiences of sexual torture left them with profoundly serious gynaecological and reproductive health needs and the same Women's International Peace Centre intervention project concluded: 'Since women were sexually targeted during the war, many of the crimes against them resulted in the damage of their reproductive organs or problems with sexually transmitted diseases, including AIDS'.

The findings contained in our intervention report were presented at a conference in Kampala, which I was delighted to attend. Women who we had interviewed powerfully spoke out about their conflict-related experiences. Although the study was well-received, proposals for services for these conflict-torture survivors were not funded. I was struck by the significant and yet untreated health problems of the women I spoke with and the extent of their traumatic experiences. All the women I talked with had been raped and/or gang-raped and had suffered terrible reproductive and gynaecological health consequences because of their experiences. These were untreated partly due to the stigma of speaking out, but also due to the lack of attention to this issue by professionals.

I was immensely proud to be part of this research, which led to one report and two journal publications (*Isis-WICCE, 1999; Liebling, 2004; 2007*). Determined to make a difference, I started campaigning to raise attention for the needs of women conflict survivors through James Plaskitt Esquire, my local MP at the time in the UK. I was incredibly pleased to be called to the vice-chancellor's office at university to receive a fax. This was from Clare Short, who was the International Development Minister in the UK. She promised to raise the issues of women conflict survivors and their needs with her department. She also mentioned that her department was engaging civil society and the Ministry of Health in taking forward our research recommendations.

Further, she reported that her department was aware of the work by African Psycare Research Organisation (APRO), of which I was a co-founding member. Following my subsequent meeting with Taaka Awori, Assistant Development Advisor for DFID in Uganda, there began to be streams of funding for violence against women internationally, which I felt was partly due to my concerted efforts to raise these issues. I felt a very warm glow at this news, and felt my hard work was resulting in positive change for those women who had trusted and confided in our team. The funding extended internationally, and this was particularly rewarding to hear.

Whilst working at the university, I established a good circle of friends in Uganda who I met with socially and in cafés in Kampala. I would also go out drinking with them in the evenings, frequently getting lifts home with Topher Kizza on his motorbike. I got on well with a young man, Fred, who was sharing our house and conducting research with butterflies. He was shy, but we went out together sometimes and had fun. We became close, as friends. Sometime later, after we had returned to the UK, I received a beautiful postcard from him and was pleased he was thinking about me.

On one of the trips to Eastern Busoga, Uganda, a woman anthropologist asked if she could travel with me to see the music. So, one weekend, I hired a much 'clapped-out' car, and we went to Iganga District. After the amazing performance, we said our goodbyes and headed back to Kampala, stopping in Jinja, the source of the Nile, for lunch by the lake. When we left after lunch and started driving, there was a huge hill to climb, and suddenly we started rolling backwards down the hill. Just as I thought we would end up at the bottom of Lake Victoria, the *boda boda* motorcycles noticed. They ran to our rescue and pushed the car, with all our luggage, back to the top of the hill. We continued happily and safely back to Kampala.

Unfortunately, during my time working at the university, I spent several months ill and was hardly able to eat without being sick. I lost weight, and the medical doctors did not seem to know what the problem was. I was missing friends from the UK and finding the politics at the university challenging. The Ugandans were treated unfairly, and this upset me. To top it all off, the local salary I was receiving stopped for a few months due to the lecturers striking, for which I did not blame them. However, this left me feeling very vulnerable, as I could not afford to take myself to the doctors. Luckily, my mum bailed me out, otherwise I do not know what I would have done. I was starting to enjoy my work less, partly due to my illness and partly due to the university bringing in a new regulation where only staff with PhDs could supervise. I had done a master's course, not a doctorate, so I did not have a PhD.

I therefore decided to take a break back home, and as I was very touched by the women's experiences in Luwero, I thought I would apply for a PhD focused on the intervention I had been involved with. Just before I travelled home, the Ugandan medical doctor suggested it might be the malaria tablets that were making me ill. He advised I stop them, which I did.

I arrived home and my mum said, 'Oh my goodness, what on earth has happened to you?'

'I have been ill, Mum', I replied.

'But you are so thin'.

'Turns out I am sensitive to the malaria tablets. They are making me sick. I have not been able to keep my food down'.

'Thank God you've come home'.

'I have just come home to see the doctor and recover. Then I will return to Uganda'.

'We'll see about that', said my mum sternly.

However, as I was feeling so unwell, I was glad to have home comforts for a while. After a week or so, I spoke to my mum about wanting to do a PhD and she mentioned that she had a friend at a university in the Midlands. In the meantime, I visited my friend Caroline in Sheffield and went to the Women and Gender Department at a local university. I had written a few ideas about following up the Luwero study for my research. This was in very brief draft form and involved interviewing women in-depth about their experiences, the impact of these, and the consequences for health and human rights. The lecturers I met did not seem that impressed with my ideas, so I left a bit disheartened, but I enjoyed spending time seeing Caroline whilst I was there.

Following my mum's recommendations, I went to the university in the Midlands and met Caroline and the other staff. I liked the department, and Caroline was very enthusiastic. She said she could help me turn my research ideas into an Economic and Social Research Council (ESRC) funding proposal. I thought that this was truly kind of her and returned to meet her and complete the application. I look back now, thinking that if I had not met her, my life may have taken a completely different direction. I feel incredibly grateful for her support.

Shortly after the meetings, and feeling much better in terms of my health, I returned to Uganda and changed to a different malaria medication. This one suited me much better. After a couple of months, I received a message to go to the vice-chancellor's office because I had received a fax. I went very excitedly and found that the fax was from Caroline, congratulating me on getting ESRC funding to start my PhD. I was incredibly sad to leave Uganda, but also knew that I would return soon for my PhD research.

I flew back to the UK, having said goodbye to all my lovely Ugandan friends. I started a job in Yorkshire while I was waiting to start my PhD. I lodged with Caroline in Sheffield and worked for about six months at a low-security unit for women in Yorkshire. Although women were treated much better, it triggered traumatic memories from the high-security hospital. I was, therefore, glad to start my PhD part-time. I commuted from Sheffield to the Midlands initially, which was a struggle. I did this for a couple of months before I found myself falling asleep while driving on the motorway and decided that enough was enough. I then moved to be nearer to the university, glad to leave my employment at the women's secure unit behind.

Twelve

Cuban Rum, Dodging Rubber Bullets, and a Wedding

After a few months of doing my PhD full-time I realised I missed working life, so I applied for a job in the health service. I was successful in getting an interview with a health service trust to work in Coventry. I was offered a part-time post as a clinical psychologist working in adult mental health services and decided to move to Leamington Spa. I initially lived in a basement flat on a lovely wide street with Edwardian-style houses. I joined the local samba group and soon met Sebastian and Ali. I became quick friends with them both.

Ali had just left her husband and needed a distraction. One day, I saw flights advertised for Cuba in the *Guardian*, which were ridiculously cheap. I said to Ali, 'Do you fancy a trip to Cuba?'

The offer was for an all-inclusive week in Havana. About two months later, we set off excitedly and stayed by the sea in a hotel with a pool. Both Ali and I love swimming, so the pool was a bonus. We had a brilliant holiday, and

Left to right: Ali and Me in Cuba with Che Guevara Hats

each chose an activity for alternate days. I was excited to find live Santora Cuban music and buy musical instruments, whilst Ali suggested galleries and a visit to the cemetery, where we saw Che Guevara's grave.

During the trip, we hired a car to visit a cigar and rum factory, as well as the beautiful Sierra Maestra Mountains, where Fidel Castro hid before the Cuban revolution. I was happy to drive, as I had done so before in African countries. We had a near miss due to the confusion of driving on the wrong side of the road and found ourselves driving up the exit leading off a main road, somehow. Luckily, there were no cars coming in the opposite direction, so we soon navigated our way to safety. The cigar factory was interesting and the mountains stunning. We stopped in the foothills, surrounded by their beauty. The air felt very fresh and there were beautiful flowers, although the land was dry.

On our return journey to Havana, we stopped at the rum factory and bought two bottles each to take home. In the evening of our last night, we decided to go out to the clubs and enjoy the nightlife. Unfortunately, Ali ran out of money, so we went to the very splendid Hotel Nacional, where famous guests had stayed, including the writer, Graham Greene. We could only afford to share a plate of chips. Afterwards, we headed off to a great bar with free live Cuban music and danced to the Latin beats until the early hours. The next day, we boarded the aeroplane to return to Birmingham and to our surprise received two free bottles of rum each to add to our collection. We clanked our way through Birmingham airport with several bottles of rum and musical instruments in our hand luggage and were relieved not to be stopped by the airport staff.

I soon settled in Leamington Spa and made friends in the samba band. We rehearsed on Thursdays and Sundays, and I enjoyed playing *caixa*, the snare drum, initially. We had great performances and always excited the crowds, who danced wildly to our rhythms. We also dressed up and played at the Leamington Peace Festival.

Although I left the samba band for a few years to focus on African music and then a choir, I returned around 2021. I play *timba*, the Brazilian hand-drum, and love performing and socialising with the group. In 2022, Sol Samba in Oxford invited the band to perform at Notting Hill Carnival. It was extremely exciting, and following several rehearsals, a few of us headed off to London for the event. Brazilian drummers and dancers would join us. We were also using our performance to make a protest about climate change and the importance of recycling for the environment.

Samba band performers and me (fourth from left) in costumes for Notting Hill

To do this, we made our costumes out of recycled crisp packets. I had some help from a Ugandan tailor who delighted in the experience of designing my outfit and making a fabulous Brazilian hat out of crisp packets, recycled bottles, and raffia. The carnival itself was outstanding and very lively with the most amazing costumes I had ever seen. The procession for more than ten hours a day was exhausting, but it was a very enjoyable and rewarding

Maxilla Social Club rehearsal venue for Notting Hill in recycled crisp packet costumes (Seda on the left, myself on the right)

event. Unfortunately, we had to leave before the end and struggled through the crowds, feeling we might be crushed to death. Eventually, after finding our way to some space, I saw several police and ambulances. The police were carrying evidence bags, so I knew there had been an incident. I saw later in the news that a musician had been shot, and I felt incredibly sad that such a beautiful cultural event was marred by this crime.

I left the samba group to set up a Ugandan traditional music and performance group. I had brought the Ugandan 21-key embaire back to my house and had a stand made. I managed to obtain lottery funding for my friend and Ugandan musician Seby to teach Ugandan embaire to the local community in Leamington Spa. This included teaching to performance level, as well as the other traditional instruments and dancing.

Our performing group was named 'Embaire Strikes Back' after the *Star Wars* film. We performed at several festivals and events, including for the Queen at the Jubilee celebrations at Westminster Abbey. We also performed at the 25-year anniversary of the World Wildlife Foundation in London, together with other musicians including Brian Adams, Peter Andre, Kiki Dee, and Elton John. Our performance was right at the start, and the actor Martin Clunes introduced us. He looked surprised and a bit embarrassed when I bumped into him as we were rushing off stage, when I said, 'You are brilliant in *Doc Martin*'. Although he looked surprised, I felt pleased I had been bold enough to tell him.

My PhD was entitled *Gendered Analysis of the Experiences of Ugandan Women War Survivors* (*Liebling-Kalifani, 2009; 2010*). It also addressed the health and human rights implications, and the course was going well. However, I found the first year incredibly challenging in a Women and Gender Department where some members could be critical of psychologists at times. I made friends on the course and in the law department. I found having supervisors from different disciplines a challenge sometimes, as they approached the research from different perspectives. Despite this I looked forward to the fieldwork in Uganda, and soon I left the UK to live in Uganda for seven months in 2001 to conduct my fieldwork.

Initially, I stayed at Makerere University and studied Luganda language, which is the language of the Baganda ethnic group, and the language spoken in Luwero where I would be conducting my fieldwork interviews. After three months of language lessons, I travelled to Luwero with my Ugandan driver. I enjoyed the scenery on the journey. The earth was so beautifully red, the sky so blue, and the land so green, being full of banana plantations. At one point we passed a tank at a place called Matugga and I asked my driver what it was doing there. He explained it remained there after the Luwero bush wars. This was interesting to me, as I was studying the long-term impact of the Luwero conflict, which took place in 1981-1986. I stayed with a female member of parliament in Luwero town. Women's Peace International Centre had linked me to her. I discovered that she was representing the opposition, and it was soon coming to election time in Uganda, so it was a very unstable period. To reassure me, she explained that she had a guard at her house for safety reasons, as she knew she could be targeted due to her political activities. It was a comfortable house, and I had a small room with a mosquito net and ate in the evenings with herself and her family. I recall that I did not eat very well, as I was anxious about the political situation and getting my fieldwork done successfully.

I travelled with the driver in our small pick-up truck from Luwero to the villages where we would be working. The MP from the district, Victoria Mwaka, had kindly contacted the women's groups she worked with and agreed to be interviewed. Women's International Peace Centre had also linked me to Margaret Nassozi, who would be my research assistant, together with my driver, who would be the male research assistant for those survivors who preferred to speak with a man. We worked in five parishes in the district of Luwero and I conducted focus groups and individual interviews with volunteers in each parish. It was hectic and exhausting, as we carried out several interviews a day in Luganda with Margaret and my driver interpreting.

Women and men conflict survivors were pleased to see me and open up about their experiences. It was very emotional at times, but conducting interviews in groups was helpful for the process, as the women and men trusted each other. They met in their groups outside of our research so that they could continue supporting each other. This was the value of using a participatory approach, whereby the research would also empower and build the local organisations and communities. We worked in separate men's and women's groups to help with discussing difficult and sensitive experiences, including rape, SGBV and torture.

I also interviewed key informants in Luwero who had supported conflict survivors, including human rights activists, justice organisations, health workers, local and religious leaders, and community-based government and non-government organisations. I got to know people in Luwero well, and one leader took me to see the skulls of the people who had died in the district during the conflict. When he removed the memorial stone, I saw countless skulls. It was very touching and heart-breaking to see and hear how people had suffered.

At weekends I would travel back to Kampala, and the women I interviewed would produce a liquid in an empty bottle of water. When I asked what it was, they told me it was *waragi*, a gin made from bananas, which was very lethal. Friends in Kampala would laugh when I shuddered at its strength, and suggested we should use it to start the barbecue, which it ignited very well. I reflected on how kind it was for the women to make it for me; I took it as a sign of appreciation for listening and validating their experiences.

As the fieldwork progressed, the political situation became more volatile. The atmosphere became extremely frightening. It culminated in an incident when I returned to Kampala. As I tried to get into the entrance to the university, I saw there was a fire. I managed to get into the campus through a side entrance, but wondered if I was doing the right thing. I could hear what I eventually found to be students demonstrating. I saw hundreds of angry protesters all over the university campus as I made my way back to my room. They were being pursued by the army, and I could hear bullets in the distance. I felt very frightened.

When I arrived at our house, Fred arrived out of breath, saying: 'Quick, Helen, go inside before you are attacked too'.

I noticed that Fred was white as a sheet and shaking all over. 'My goodness, what happened?' I asked.

'The students have been rioting all over the campus. I was in my lab, and they threw a sharp metal object through the window. Luckily, I ducked, and it missed me. Otherwise, I could be dead'.

I hardly had time to utter these words before I saw students running into our drive, the sound of bullets remarkably close. I also heard and smelled gas everywhere. I knew then that we were in terrible danger.

'Quick, let's hide in my room', I said.

We ran into my room, shut the door, and cowered behind my bed, feeling very scared but trying not to make a sound so that the crowds would not know we were there. Luckily for us, the crowd moved past and went to the Vice-Chancellor's house. After what seemed like forever, the rioting ceased.

Shortly afterwards, a friend came to check on us and we found out that two students had been killed during the political violence, but it was publicised as a domestic incident so the government would not be blamed. The government had sent in the army, who had authorised the use of bullets and tear gas. We then discovered that the Vice-Chancellor's son, who lived next door to us, had been shot and taken to Mulago Hospital. He survived, but I was acutely aware that rubber bullets could also kill. After this incident,

I became increasingly concerned for my safety, as burning tyres were often found in the road after riots and more fires were started at the entrance to Makerere University.

In Luwero, ironically, the political instability meant that the conflict survivors I spoke to wanted to discuss their previous experiences in respect to the current situation. They told me it was helpful to speak with someone from outside Uganda who was not politically involved. I thought this was an interesting perception, as in fact I was extremely interested in politics. However, this impression clearly assisted the research.

Although the research interviews were going well, there were increasing threats of attack on the woman I was lodging with. One day, the health workers from Luwero were abducted by rebels in a hostage situation and all their belongings stolen. I then decided it was all too stressful, and I flew home to wait until the elections were over. My research assistant and driver continued working but informed me while I was away that their vehicle had been broken into and some of my research equipment was stolen. Luckily, none of the research assistants were harmed.

I returned to Uganda after the elections to find it peaceful again, although it was reported that Museveni, the president of Uganda, had won by apparently rigging the elections. The opposition leader, Kizza Besigye, had fled to South Africa for safety reasons before the voting took place. I travelled back to Luwero with a new vehicle and research equipment and finished the interviews peacefully. Everyone was pleased to see me, and I was happy to have ended the research peacefully and successfully. I was also glad that those I had spoken to in my research were unharmed by the political violence.

I returned to the UK. After writing up my PhD, one supervisor suggested I was ready to submit, while the other felt I needed a further six months. By this time, I felt ready to submit and went against one of my supervisors' wishes, submitting my thesis in 2004. I had a Viva Voce, which is the oral examination to answer questions about my thesis, with two examiners – an external and internal. It was a challenge and lasted three hours. When they said that I had to revise and resubmit, I felt upset. However, when I saw what was required, I understood and did not feel so bad, and Professor Gillian Hundt helped me to make the changes and re-submit without any problems. She was incredibly supportive of me.

After my PhD had been resubmitted, I had an interview for a clinical tutor post at another Midlands university, which I was successful in obtaining. I started working there in September 2004. I recall on the day of my interview being shown around the university buildings by a Ugandan man from Information Technology. He was warm and enthusiastic, which made me feel positive about the post. Although I found some of the buildings austere, I loved the library, which was built to be ecologically friendly. I also frequented the cafés and liked the fact that the buildings were near the centre of town.

Prior to this, I had become close to Mugwisa, and we started going out with each other. I was a bit concerned at first, as he was traditionally married to a Ugandan woman and they had children, but he signed a declaration of facts to say that they had separated. We tried to obtain a visitor's permit so that he could visit me in the United Kingdom, but the British High Commission in Uganda refused, stating that he might never return. I found this very annoying, as we wanted to spend time together in the UK before getting married, to see if Mugwisa could settle there. I also found it ridiculous that the letter said he might not go back to Uganda, as he had been born and raised in Uganda and loved it very much.

We decided to get married in 2006. The first wedding was meant to take place in Jinja, but I got cold feet and did not go ahead with the ceremony. There were some inconsistencies in Mugwisa's behaviour that concerned me. My friend Ali came out to Uganda, and she was incredibly supportive, but later the problems resolved over the ex-wife, and we married in Jinja. My dad came out, which was brilliant, and we had the best party ever in the village with the old men playing endongo, Mugwisa's group playing xylophone, and some Matali Muslims playing the drums. It was a wonderful day, one of the happiest of my life, and I wore my Ugandan blue Busuti dress with pride.

Embaire performance at my wedding to Mugwisa, April 2006

Mugwisa came over to see if he could settle in the UK and set up the performing Ugandan xylophone group to teach people to play. He did this using the Awards for All Lottery Funding, then Arts Council funding, which helped to give him some employment. Initially, he was excited to be in the UK, and it was great showing him around. I recall him asking me why the sun did not have any heat, which I found amusing.

As time went on, however, he would receive telephone calls from Uganda saying that he was needed at home. He was the only boy in the extended family whose role was to care for the children, so the family were struggling without him. We started arguing, and he found being in the UK difficult. Seby, my Ugandan friend, helped me to teach the xylophone when Mugwisa went back to Uganda.

He returned after some time and we got another year's funding to continue the 'Embaire Strikes Back' group, but eventually he insisted on going back to Uganda. I did not feel that living apart was a good start to the marriage, and so I tried to get a job in Uganda. I failed in this, and so we stayed living in different countries. However, the xylophone group was doing very well. We managed to get together a group of committed people to regularly practice. We started performing at festivals, parties, and various events in the UK, and even recorded a CD.

Through my friend Rosalind, the older feminist network in South Wales decided to fundraise after I presented my PhD research. I was so pleased by this. Their group held music recitals, made and sold soup, and raised £1,500, which they sent to me. With this money, we were able to buy goats and to feed back the research in Luwero. We gave every research participant interviewed during my PhD a goat.

The idea was that every woman would have her own sustainable income through owning her own goat. The goats were also given to male survivors I had interviewed, so the income would assist their families. At the workshop, my research assistant Margaret, who was part of a theatre group, also took the main themes of my research and presented them through a performance, which included music and dancing in the local language of Luganda.

The funding also enabled me to organise a medical intervention in Luwero, to bring all the male and female research participants for urgent treatment to a medical centre in Luwero Town. By doing this, I was also able to highlight the pressing need for a gynaecologist in Luwero by taking a gynaecologist from Kampala to Luwero to treat affected women. This was reported in the Ugandan newspapers and highlighted the need for this initiative.

Left to right: Mugwisa and my dad

At around the same time, my dad was serving as the international officer in Rotary International and his organisation agreed to partly fund the construction of a well in Luwero. They joined with the Rotary organisation in Luwero, and we collaborated with the engineers to build a bore well at the girl's school in Kikamulo. We hoped the community around would benefit. I remember the engineers explaining that the water table was exceptionally low, and that they had to drill eighty metres down to reach the water. I was excited when my dad came out to Luwero for my wedding and to open the bore well, to a great party with dancing and music. The local organisers also had a plaque made in my dad's honour, a truly kind gesture. I was incredibly pleased that my dad came to Uganda, as he was the only person in my family to do so, and it meant a great deal to me. He took it all in his stride and got on well with everyone he met.

I was later successful in obtaining a small research grant from the university to follow up and conduct an evaluation of these projects established through my PhD recommendations. I therefore returned to Luwero in 2005 to interview participants about the success and sustainability of the clean water, medical intervention, and income-generation projects I had established. This research concluded that all the projects had assisted conflict survivors in their recovery journey and the income-generating project with the goats had led to sustainable income for those concerned (*Liebling-Kalifani, 2009*). This made me immensely proud.

Thirteen

The Power of Writing in the Fight for 'Justice'

I continued working at the university and managed to move from my role as clinical tutor to research tutor, which I preferred. It would involve more opportunities for research-related work. I wished to follow up and disseminate my PhD as much as possible, and secured funding to feed back the research findings to the International Rescue Committee for Torture Survivors in Copenhagen, as well as the Department of Women, Gender, and Health at the World Health Organisation in Geneva. Shortly afterwards, I was successful in obtaining funding from the British Academy to run a workshop on female conflict survivors with Women's International Peace Centre at the International Women's Summit in Nairobi.

I started collaborating with a colleague who supported my work. I also divorced Mugwisa. This was a long, drawn-out process that took several years. Although it felt like the right decision at the time, there was something gnawing at me about my relationship with Uganda. With faith in a better future, I persisted with the support of friends.

I was extremely excited at this time to be invited by Women's International Peace Centre to take part in a consultancy in Monrovia, Liberia to plan an intervention, and to provide training for professionals to give medical and psychological treatment for conflict survivors. I was so excited to fly to Liberia and loved it – the location on the coast was beautiful. We had a few days in the capital, Monrovia, to meet, and I was struck by the number of women police in the city. I soon learned that the head of state had done an excellent job of engendering the police force there. I returned some months later to adapt the training manual, which we had developed based on research conducted in northern Uganda. I then returned to Liberia to participate in training on the border of Côte d'Ivoire.

After flying to Monrovia, I met Juliet from Women's International Peace Centre, and we both prepared the training and packed all the medical supplies to take with us to Harper. As my co-authored article *Liebling et al. (2011)* describes:

> *Fourteen years of armed conflict in Liberia resulted not only in the destruction of Liberia's social and economic infrastructure, but high levels of brutality by all factions. These included widespread killings, rape, sexual assault, abduction, torture, forced labour, and recruitment of child soldiers. As a result, . . . the population is suffering from a wide range of psychological effects, alcohol and drug-related addiction, surgical problems, and for women, urgent gynaecological issues. Yet the broken-down health system of Liberia struggles to respond to the needs of survivors of sexual abuse. There are few health centres or adequately trained and employed health workers to deal with the overwhelming levels of health needs.*

In response to these issues, we assembled a team to train seventy different professionals from four counties in Liberia, to support and treat conflict survivors. We were mindful that many of the professionals we were training had also suffered badly during the conflict period and were, therefore, survivors as well. Through our collaborative research, WIPC and I then worked with a local Liberian team to provide emergency medical and psychological treatment to conflict-affected communities, train local health workers, build capacity, and at the same time, highlight the impact of conflict on women. We also submitted articles for the newspapers and interviews that were broadcast live on Liberian radio stations.

In line with our research recommendations, WIPC obtained a European Union grant from the Dutch Government of the Millennium Development Goal 3 Fund, to conduct emergency medical interventions in two of the countries where we had carried out research. Maryland and Grand Kru in Liberia were chosen, due to their remote and under-developed infrastructure, their lack of medical services, and their heavy burden of gynaecological and psychological problems revealed during the study.

The training and intervention in Harper aimed to provide specialised healthcare for women war survivors, deliver reproductive health kits to rural health units, and build the capacity of local health workers in the management of reproductive and surgical complications through surgical camps. It also aimed to bring in primary health workers to provide psychological support. Finally, we intended to pilot a training manual for health workers in the recognition, assessment, and management of the psychological, reproductive, and surgical health consequences of conflict.

Members of our team travelled to Harper, where we would conduct the training by road. We were lucky to be able to fly from Monrovia. I excitedly went to the tiny airport just outside Monrovia with a few of our team and helped to load the medical supplies onto the conveyer belt. I noticed that there were UN helicopters flying, and a man from the UN started speaking to me.

I explained our work and the reason we were flying to Harper by a small aeroplane. He said, 'You are probably very wise. It is safer, as the helicopters often get caught in the bushes and crash'. Although slightly alarmed by his remark, I felt reassured, and when I saw the Minister of Gender herself climb onto the small aeroplane, I felt happy. There were only about twelve seats on the aircraft, but it was a beautiful, calm sunny day, and it was an amazing flight along the coast of Liberia with stunning views. I could see from the window that the landing infrastructure was minimal, and the bush unpassable. I also heard that due to the torrential rains, the roads were often difficult to navigate and that bridges often collapsed due to poor maintenance.

We arrived safely and went to our accommodation in a church mission, where we would also conduct the training. We shared the drinks and food between us, and I remember eating rice and an extraordinarily spicy sauce. This gave the Liberians a laugh. The heat was stifling, and I sweated continually, but was happy to be conducting such excellent work. I got to know the participants and other trainers, and during our few breaks, we went for walks along the coast. I was shocked by the sight of graves lining the road, and one of the Liberians told me that this was due to the country running out of spaces to bury all those killed during the conflict. Seeing the graves really brought home the reality of how devastated Liberia had been.

The training was delivered at a workshop for health workers carried out in Harper, Maryland County, in May 2009. A total of forty-nine participants – twenty-four women and twenty-five men – attended the training. This emphasised an integrated approach, which included counselling and management of psychological trauma, sexual and reproductive health, gender-based violence, human rights, and professional standards in healthcare. As the trainees were also conflict survivors, the training included individual and group counselling to model a way of professionals supporting themselves, which they could continue to use in their own communities.

We delivered urgently needed drugs and equipment to twelve health centres and two hospitals. The trained health workers, social workers, and community leaders conducted screenings of survivors. A total of 1,076 survivors – 685 women and 391 men – were seen for assessments by the team. A screening questionnaire identified the following conditions: epilepsy, mental health disorders, infertility, pelvic inflammatory diseases, fibroids, vesico-vaginal fistula (VVF; an abnormal connection between the bladder and vagina which results in uncontrolled leaking of urine), genital prolapses, hernias, hydroceles, enlarged and elongated breasts, swellings, malaria and fevers, malnourishment in children, and urinary tract infections.

The surgery focussed on sexual and reproductive health complications, including VVFs, uterine fibroids, genital prolapses, and infertility problems. Some survivors had more than one surgical condition that needed treatment. A total of 207 survivors – sixty women and 147 men, ranging from one to ninety years old – benefitted from the surgical camp.

Due to the enormous numbers who accessed the services, the medical consultants and other staff volunteered extra hours. The heavy rains and the poor road infrastructure were a key challenge. It is also important to note that previous health programmes in this area had focussed on men, and most women assumed that this was still the case. Once women saw their fellow women benefitting from the programme, they came for treatment.

However, due to limited funding, there were restrictions on what could be achieved. Ill mental and physical health was still predominant, and there were high rates of loss and grief, physical, sexual, and psychological torture, and intimate partner violence. Although men were also affected, the majority of those who reported psychological problems were women.

After a few days, one of the Liberian women trainers asked, 'Have you been using Dettol to wash with?'

'No, should I have been?' I replied.

The Liberian woman looked very worried and ran off. She very shortly returned and said, 'Please wash with this immediately, and make sure you put it in all the water you wash with from now on'.

'Why?' I asked her, feeling concerned by now.

'Well, I am sure it is nothing to worry about, but the water comes directly from the sewerage and the cleaning system is not what it should be'.

'Oh dear', I said, and the woman ran off before I could ask any more awkward questions.

It was then that I noticed I had developed lumps on my neck and was concerned I might get ill. I was also not eating or drinking much. Being vegetarian, I decided to go to the market to see if I could find anything to eat. I could only find a few small fish, and as I do not eat fish, this was not helpful.

At the end of the week's training, we had a fabulous party. I had a Liberian dress made, and there was Liberian traditional music and dancing. I love my dress, which has beautiful red and orange colours, a fabulous design with circular patterns, and trousers underneath. I still have it and wear it with pride, although it has been repaired several times. The training in Harper had gone well, and we left incredibly happy. However, when I returned to the United Kingdom, I felt sick and went to the GP, who announced I had a kidney infection. They sent me for a scan. I then found out that I had cysts on my right kidney, and the GP recommended I drink plenty of water. I was unwell for a while, but after drinking a lot of water and a course of antibiotics, I recovered well.

In 2008, I received further funding from the Royal Society and British Academy to present two papers on the research and consultancy I had been involved with in Liberia. This led to the awarding of a prize for outstanding research for my presentation on Liberian conflict survivors at the Sexual Violence Research Initiative Conference in Johannesburg. I was immensely honoured when I gave the paper describing what the team of fifty Liberian colleagues together with WIPC had achieved. I had to make my way to the platform at the conference in front of hundreds of people for Rachel Jewkes, Chair of Sexual Violence Research Initiative, to hand me the award, which was a great moment.

I continued to collaborate with my colleague, who was a professor at the university. We obtained funding to conduct research with former child abductees in Northern Uganda. The project went well, due to his expertise in policing and justice and my expertise with survivors and health issues. After we launched the project report, I was asked to present the research at the African Union Pre-Summit on Gender Mainstreaming in Uganda. I attended the meeting and presented our research as part of a panel, which focussed on peace and reconciliation in Northern Uganda.

Mary Robinson, the former President of Southern Ireland, was present and chaired our panel. Afterwards, Ruth Ojiambo-Ochieng from WIPC introduced us. Mary Robinson said that she would like a copy of the book, as she and two other women were taking a helicopter to meet Yoweri Museveni, the president of Uganda (*Liebling & Baker, 2010a*). This was to discuss the recommendations of the Summit Meeting with him. I was very honoured to be asked for my research, and gladly gave her my final copy of the book. She later returned with Victoria Mwaka, president of WIPC, and told the conference that the recommendations of my research were discussed with

President Museveni, who agreed to implement them through the Ministry of Health and his security advisors. I was so incredibly pleased and grateful for my colleague to all his support in making the research so impactful (*Liebling & Baker, 2010a; 2010b; Liebling, 2012*).

In 2010, I received a grant from the university to work with the Gender Research Unit in Pretoria with Rachel Jewkes and Stellenbosch University in Cape Town. I was pleased to accept this opportunity and spent two weeks living in Pretoria and working with Rachel and her team at the Medical Research Institute. I got to know the staff, especially Laura and Rachel. Laura took me to buy a woolly hat and gloves, as it snowed for the first time in thirty years in South Africa, and everyone ran out of their offices to see the spectacular sight. It was so cold that I slept in my clothes with my small heater on.

Rachel took me to a seminar on gender-based violence with school children, which took place in a women's prison in Johannesburg. It was an interesting setting, and I read about all the women who had been abused in prison during the Apartheid era. I then went to work in Cape Town for two weeks and got to know a psychiatrist at Stellenbosch University who asked me to present a seminar at the Gender, Health, and Justice Unit at the University of Cape Town. I liked the University of Cape Town; I liked the staff, and we went for a drink and food after the seminar. We also talked about how we might work together, which was extremely exciting.

Clarissa's cousin Walter lived in Cape Town, and he invited me to go flying. I was excited about this opportunity and made my way to the north of the city. Luckily, it was a beautiful sunny day, and I got in the back of a double glider. Another small plane was in front, which helped us lift off and then let us go. It was amazing to float above the mountains, which were covered in snow and stunningly beautiful. There was no engine noise as we drifted along. It was an incredible experience.

Walter asked me if I wanted to have a go at steering, and I happily said yes. I managed to steer for a while and then he asked, 'Do you want to see what else the glider can do?' I assented without quite realising what I had let myself in for.

Walter turned the glider so that it tilted to the right and then to the left. Then he tilted ninety degrees down to the ground before quickly turning one-eighty degrees to go straight up into the sky. I was, at this point, starting to feel extremely sick and dizzy. I told him and he landed the glider. By this time, I was feeling very unwell, and he lifted me out of the glider, plonked me on the floor, and advised me to put my head between my knees. He said

106

that I would be fine in a little while. After about twenty minutes of sitting on the landing strip with my head between my legs, I stood up and was delighted to see a red bishop; a beautiful black bird with a stunningly red head. I felt much better and drove back excitedly to Cape Town.

I finished my work, having written a publication and a large research grant, which I was hoping to submit once I returned to the UK. I was sad to leave Cape Town and South Africa, but I had a feeling I would be back before too long.

Fourteen

Saving Babies and Navigating Security Threats

I continued to work on research grants and obtained funding to interview refugees in Coventry. I was extremely excited to be selected to write a British Academy grant entitled *Women who bear children through rape during conflict: stigma, health, and justice responses in eastern Congo* in 2011. I led the writing of the grant, and Rachel Jewkes in South Africa connected me to Henny Slegh, a psychotherapist and researcher living in Kigali, Rwanda. She recommended we worked with Benoit Ruratotoye, a Congolese clinical psychologist, at the Institute of Mental Health in Goma, Eastern DRC (Democratic Republic of Congo). I was excited after an epic struggle to successfully obtain my visa, but also nervous about travelling to do research on a sensitive issue in Eastern DRC, which had a reputation for being the 'rape capital of the world'.

I flew to Kigali, where I was greeted by Benoit and Henny at the airport. They then dropped me off at my accommodation. We met the following day, discussed the research, and agreed that, due to the security situation, we should base ourselves in Kigali, Rwanda, and travel to DRC by road for work Mondays to Fridays. Henny knew a good hotel where we could stay safely. We set off on our journey with excitement. When we arrived at the border to DRC, we had a fabulous welcome and proceeded to our hotel. I reflected on how different this was from the reception in Rwanda, which had been more serious.

The next day, we got up early to meet Benoit and the team, including our driver. I was surprised to learn that, to conduct the research, we had to visit the mayor of Goma and pay a bribe, as there was no ethics committee in this region. When I objected, Benoit looked at me quizzically and commented that if I wanted to complete the research, I had no choice. After a discussion with Henny, we agreed I needed to take Benoit's advice on this. I reluctantly gave him the money and told him to meet the mayor himself, as I wanted nothing to do with it.

Following this, we were able to start our interviews. I was moved by how friendly everyone was in Goma, which was also incredibly beautiful, with vibrant colours, bustling streets, and a volcano and beautiful lake in the distance. This is when the road in Goma struck so hard with its terrible, black and rugged terrain, which was exceedingly difficult to walk on.

We went on to meet with groups of women and children who had been conceived following rape. Eighty percent of those who wished to speak with us were young girls, and I found it harrowing to hear the words of these suicidal, young, extremely poor yet resilient people. We spoke in groups about their experiences. This was important, as it meant the girls had a support structure during the project. It was the most upsetting research I had conducted, and I relied on the support of my colleagues to get me through.

After the first week, we made our way back to Rwanda and enjoyed a weekend in Kigali. During the second week, we worked in rural Bweremana, about three hours from Goma. The road was so bad that I had a migraine every day, which made the research very tough on top of the distress I felt. I consoled myself with the knowledge that the girls were volunteering to speak, and if their voices were heard, maybe it would effect a positive change in them and in the services provided. However, I was careful to never promise this.

There were elements of the research that I could not control, despite being the lead. Most people were used to bribes, and I had to keep explaining that there was a clear budget we needed to stick to. This was often ignored, and it was a constant struggle to keep the finances in line, which I managed notwithstanding the stress. I spent every night before bed frantically trying to sort through our grant spending. Sometimes the power would go off, and I would struggle under the mosquito net with a torch and my laptop, trying to balance the books. I am sure this played a part in the migraines I was experiencing.

As well as interviewing women and girls, we interviewed health and justice service provider professionals and services that supported women and girls who had been raped. I interviewed professionals working for a very impressive organisation called Synergie de Femmes. They were a non-government organisation who assisted women survivors of SGBV to seek justice and gain support and treatment. They were very noble, and a lot of their staff – who covered the Northern Kivu province – worked for nothing out of the goodness of their heart. I was full of admiration for their commitment, but also empathetic of their very tough situation. They worked with inadequate support structures, poor salary and living conditions, and

110

were often survivors of SGBV themselves. Their role entailed great risks. Eastern DRC, I was told by my Congolese colleagues, was controlled by several rebel leaders. Those who supported survivors became targets as well.

After we left DRC, I felt exhausted, but I was happy that the research had gone well. I transcribed and analysed the interviews and started writing up the project. During this time, I had an interview with the Stephen Lewis Foundation for a consultant position with a Ugandan team at Panzi Hospital in South Kivu, to support the staff who were burnt out. Panzi Hospital was a specialist hospital that provided care and support to women and girls who had been raped. I was successful in obtaining the consultancy and flew to Uganda to meet the Ugandan team to discuss our mission. When I arrived at Birmingham Airport, I received a voicemail on my telephone. A very threatening male voice spoke in what sounded like Kiswahili, a Congolese language. I was genuinely concerned and saved the message to play to my Ugandan colleagues.

When I did, they said it sounded like a threat to me from Eastern DRC, and they advised me to go to the High Commission. There, I spoke to one of the representatives and explained what had happened.

'Can I listen to the message?' the man said. He then looked concerned and said, 'Well, it sounds like a threat from Eastern DRC, as it is in Kiswahili language. We cannot advise you to travel there for work, and if you do, we will not assist you if you have any problems.'

I dragged myself, very disheartened and disappointed, from the High Commission, feeling that the representative's negative response gave me no choice. I wanted the mission to go well, so I reluctantly decided to instead travel home to the UK. I was terribly upset, as I had wanted to give back to people affected by the conflict following my research. This felt like the ethical thing to do, but at the same time, I did not wish to bring problems. Feeling very deflated by the experience and concerned for my own safety, I reported the incident to the police.

Sometime later, the director of Synergy de Femmes contacted me. She asked me if I was safe and said that her case was now at the International Criminal Court (ICC) in The Hague. She told me that after I had left, the UK BBC had interviewed her on the radio about the situation of survivors in Eastern DRC, and she had named some of the rebels who had committed these abuses. Her safety was then severely compromised, and she had needed to leave DRC immediately. Luckily, she was connected to the president of DRC, and he was able to fly her to safety. When she contacted me, she had lodged her concerns to the ICC and was living in Europe. She explained how after the interview was broadcast, rebels had ransacked her house and taken personal items, including her mobile. She was later informed that the police thought the rebels had threatened all the contacts in her telephone book, including me. I was sure at that moment that I had made the right decision not to work in Eastern DRC at that time, as I could have put the mission at risk and/or been taken hostage just for the rebels to prove a point. The Ugandan mission went well, but soon after the team left, the bodyguard of Dr Denis Mukwege – the medical doctor, gynaecologist, and founder of Panzi Hospital – was killed, and Dr Mukwege also had to be flown to Geneva for his own safety.

Following my return to the UK, I was successful in obtaining a consultancy to work with a group of women at Social Development Direct, an organisation based in London. The project was to assess the value of counselling services delivered by the International Planned Parenthood Federation in rural locations in Colombia. The health service was supportive and gave me twelve days to work on the project with the proviso that the income would go towards the organisation. I was happy about this. I wanted the experience, which was more important to me than the money. I helped the team to design the research but did not travel to Colombia, as two Spanish-speaking colleagues were already selected. The project went well, and resulted in us designing a manual which could be used in all the International Planned Parenthood Federation (IPPF) clinics worldwide. A great achievement.

Following this, I was successful in receiving British Academy funding to investigate conflict survivors' experiences of trauma services in northern Uganda, and Rwanda and their implications for mental health policy and legislation. I collaborated with a barrister from London and Kitgum Women's Peace Initiative (KIWEPI), a women's non-government organisation established by WIPC, and worked in Northern Uganda with women and WIPC and survivors. We provided support and income-generating activities for women and girls and connected them to essential services, including reproductive healthcare and treatment.

The project was a challenge. I was working with a colleague who I had not met prior, although we had spoken on the telephone. The research went well in Northern Uganda, but after carrying out interviews in Rwanda, I was contacted by a minister who prevented us from publishing our findings. This was a real blow, and a situation that I felt ethically and morally bad about. Survivors and service-providers who were also survivors of the genocide had poured their hearts out to us, and we were unable to publish the findings and give justice to their narratives.

At an African study conference shortly afterwards, I met two women from Barcelona who were doing creative writing projects. They were interested in my work with conflict survivors and we decided to pool together to write a funding proposal for training WIPC staff in creative writing to improve their interventions for survivors. We were successful in obtaining funding from UAB Solidarity Foundation in 2014 and spent a week with WIPC, training their staff in creative writing. This also led to an online publication called *In/visible Traumas: Writing to Build Peace* (*Liebling, 2018*), where I reflected personally on my research with conflict survivors and the use of creative methods in research. This, I felt, was a critical point in my life where I became interested in creative writing. I wanted to use it to effect positive changes for survivors, but also to create a space to reflect on my own decisions.

In 2015, I was awarded funding from the health service to conduct projects to assess the health and well-being of refugees, as well as the staff who worked with them, in the Midlands. I did this with a colleague and two trainees, who presented their findings at a conference on Refugees Journeys' *Well-Being, Resilience and Justice in Coventry* issue in 2016. We also obtained funding from the British Psychological Society and City of Sanctuary for this. The event went very well, and as part of the conference planning group, we developed policy recommendations that were disseminated and discussed with the Houses of Parliament. I was delighted the research had resulted in this impact.

I was also starting to collaborate with Professor Hazel Barrett at the university, who helped me supervise a trainee's project on female genital mutilation. The trainee clinical psychologist did very well and published all three chapters of her thesis, which made me enormously proud. Hazel and I then submitted a research proposal together with Professor Lillian Artz, the director of the Gender, Health, and Justice Research Unit at the University of Cape Town. This was titled *Sexual and Gender-Based Violence and Torture Experiences of Sudanese Refugees in northern Uganda: Health and Justice Responses*. We were pleased to receive funding from the British Academy and Leverhulme Trust. This was extremely exciting, as I had never been to a refugee settlement. Now we would have the opportunity.

Going through ethics took about nine months, as we needed to go through the Midlands University, Gulu University in Uganda, Uganda National Science and Technology, the Refugee Department in the Office of the President, Kampala, and the ethics committee of the University of Cape Town. I managed to get the research team an extension for the research so that we could make up for this delay. We travelled with our lovely driver Emmanuel to Northern Uganda and stayed in Adjumani, where we worked for the first week. We needed approval from the commander of the settlements, so we first visited there and were made to feel welcome. We were then introduced by the commanders to the Refugee Welfare Councils, which comprised of women and men refugees from South Sudan. They were able to raise any grievances with the settlement commanders as well as support each other with challenges. We recruited a female and a male interpreter through the Refugee Welfare Council, who were incredibly supportive of our research and assisted us to recruit volunteers. I interviewed the women refugee survivors in groups, and Hazel interviewed the men.

The interviews went well, and after one week we drove to Bidi Bidi, the second largest refugee settlement in the world. We arrived in a very rundown town where we dropped our bags off at the best hotel. This was a challenge, as the roads were very bumpy and almost impassable in places. Some staff seemed very fed up and were unresponsive to requests we made. The team felt the rooms were not up to standard and there were frequent power cuts. The food was limited and, on one night, flying insects came into the dining room, which we ended up eating together with the food. This was very off-putting.

One night, we went to the town and found tasty food, although being a vegetarian, I ended up with just chips and avocado. Although we were able to laugh about the trials we faced, they were frustrating and stressful for the team. I played my Ugandan thumb piano to cheer us all up.

After a night at the hotel, we drove to Bidi Bidi and met with the commander, who gave us approval to collaborate with the Refugee Welfare Council to recruit volunteer refugees. Prior to starting the interviews, we had a tour of the settlement and arrived at the food distribution point, where food was distributed to refugees from trucks. We were informed that the food was delivered monthly, and twelve kilograms were given to one family member. We soon discovered that a substantial proportion of the refugees, particularly the men, were not registered, and therefore did not receive any food rations. This meant that often refugees were sharing their limited allocations of food between whole families. This was a very tough situation.

We were about to start our interviews in Bidi Bidi when I received a telephone call from a UN agency telling us not to interview refugees without attending a meeting with them first. I found this strange, as we had sent all our ethical clearance papers to the agency and had had no problems in Adjumani. I spoke to the research team, who were very perplexed, and so we drove to meet with the UN, taking Gladys, the Director of Kitgum Women's

Peace Initiative, with us. When we arrived, we were surprised not to be offered a drink, and were left in the room for some time wondering what was happening. Eventually one woman, who claimed she was the head of the organisation, returned to the room.

She had all our ethical clearance papers in front of her but started the meeting aggressively, saying, 'What gives you the right to interview our refugees?' The interrogation went on, and at one point she said, 'Well, women refugees won't be happy to speak to you, and men refugees will not talk about sexual violence'.

Hazel responded by explaining that she had interviewed several male volunteer refugee survivors in Adjumani already. This did not seem to help. Luckily, I had had the foresight to bring Gladys; I think having a Ugandan at the meeting helped a lot. Eventually, after a gruelling few hours we were informed that we could proceed. However, we were told we would have to recruit women through the UN's partners, which restrained us. We all left with the feeling that the agency was trying to stop us from conducting the research. The team felt concerned that this could be about silencing women and men survivors of SGBV and torture, and we felt extremely uncomfortable. We were angry and discussed strategic ways of dealing with these issues.

The following morning, we returned to Bidi Bidi. Hazel had to cross a river with her male interpreter to interview male survivors, as the bridge had broken down. Lilly and I interviewed women in the women's centre.

Following our interviews, we both needed the toilet, so we went out to the pit latrines in the garden. I entered one and when I pulled my underwear down, a huge, luminous green snake shot in and started whirling around the latrine like a maniac. It was long and thin, and I did not much like the look of it in my position. I shouted for Lilly to shut her door, but it was too late. The persistent attacker found its way through the bottom of the door into Lilly's latrine, and we both ran out screaming. Then, when we realised the snake had sped off, we both fell about laughing.

We both went back into the women's centre, still giggling with relief, and recounted the incident to the staff. One woman exclaimed, 'My goodness. You were both very lucky. That is the deadly green tree snake, and if it had bitten you, you could both be dead. The nearest anti-venom is a six-hour drive away'.

I noticed Lilly turn white as a sheet. Then my mobile started ringing. It was Kato, my Ugandan friend from Kampala. I related the story of the snake to him, and he said, 'Helen, you and your friend have had a narrow escape. I was offered a job in that area, and I only lasted two weeks before leaving, as those deadly green tree snakes kept jumping in the bus'. We went to meet Hazel, who had finished her interviews and again recounted the incident. Hazel fell about laughing and said, 'You are very lucky, thank goodness you weren't bitten'. We then found Eriab and were extremely glad to drive back to our hotel alive after our encounter.

We returned to Kampala earlier than anticipated. Hazel and I completed interviews with other key informants and government representatives in Kampala, including the Commission for Refugees. They were understandably anxious about being interviewed, as a journalist had recently written an expose about the refugee situation in Uganda. There was also an inquiry happening into corruption regarding the refugee response. This context understandably made our research a big challenge.

We returned to the UK, and I put in an application for funding to set up social enterprise projects for refugees. Hazel, Pascal, her PhD student, and I were extremely excited about being able to give back to refugees we had interviewed during the research. We returned to Uganda and the refugees were incredibly happy to see us. They put on a brilliant performance of traditional music to welcome us. As we had collaborated with refugees in groups during the research, women and men were already in their groups. Interestingly, men and women from both settlements were working together. When we went to Bidi Bidi, one of the women refugees had a very malnourished baby who would not breast-feed. She was very distressed and thought the baby would die. I remembered that I had UHT milk in our van and got some. Although my colleagues were sceptical, the refugee mother was then able to feed the baby sips of milk, and the baby appeared to pick up. We then ran the women's and men's groups, which went well.

The next day, another refugee asked me to see her baby, so I visited her hut. She put the very fragile baby in my arms. I noticed immediately that the baby's breathing was erratic. Clarissa and I left the others to run the groups and prioritised taking the baby to the clinic. The staff at the clinic knew the baby and told me in confidence that she may have had a heart condition, and that the surgery was unlikely to be available in Uganda.

She was transported to the main hospital. Clarissa and I visited the hospital in the evening. The refugee was there with her husband, and I asked if they had given the baby oxygen. She replied that there was no power, so they were unable to provide any. I was very worried and therefore spoke with the medical officer about transferring her to a better hospital. Clarissa and I left her money to assist, as we were worried the baby might die.

We returned to Uganda nine months later with my friend Clarissa and were pleased to learn that all the social enterprise groups had gone well. The refugees felt they were beneficial to their ability to earn an income, care for their families, and support each other. Refugees also showed us their social enterprise groups, and we visited the mushrooms being grown in Bidi Bidi and the soap they were making and selling. One of the refugees had established a small clinic and had treated over one thousand refugees with medical problems, which was an amazing achievement. We were also pleased to learn that the baby who had not been feeding had survived and was thriving.

Clarissa had come with us, as sadly her father had recently passed away and his family were interested in setting up a charity in his honour. We were hopeful that they might be able to use the funds to support a refugee project, which has been named the CLAMP project (*Liebling et al. 2022*). When we returned to Kampala, we met with my Ugandan colleagues as well as Interaid, who supported urban refugees. They were a priority for service provision, as they did not have the same support as those refugees in the settlements. We therefore agreed to extend Interaid services for urban refugees, and we interviewed to recruit a psychiatric clinical officer and counsellor before we left Uganda. We also gave funds to purchase a motorbike so that the staff could provide services for refugees in the rural area. We would also provide counselling through training and employing refugees as peer counsellors.

I returned in December 2020 to meet with colleagues who were running the service, and although the service had to stop for several months due to COVID, our Ugandan colleagues gave a brilliant presentation on what they had been able to provide. They also discussed re-starting the service and managed to succeed after we left.

The CLAMP refugee project is progressing well with excellent feedback from refugees, and I have managed to secure ongoing funding to continue the project, which has made me very satisfied. You can read more about this project on the global compact on refugees UNHCR website.

Fifteen

Wild Swimming through COVID to an African Future

As I reflect on my life so far, I am pleased with what I have achieved to assist conflict survivors of SGBV and torture in Africa, as well as refugee survivors in the UK and Africa. My personal goal of living in Africa has not yet come to fruition, but I hope that in the next few years, this will become a reality. I had a plan to emigrate, but two years ago this suddenly fell apart. I never understood why, and it was very traumatic. I had spent eight years looking forward to it, and this affected me very deeply. However, despite the dreadful impact of COVID, I have been able to refocus my life back towards achieving my own goals.

In March 2020, coronavirus hit the world, and I started – along with everyone else in the country – to work from home. Initially I found this relieving, as people were getting incredibly worried at work about the spreading infection. If someone coughed, it was like they had committed a major crime, and people's anxiety levels were extremely high. This led to unnecessary arguments, which I found stressful. I have always found conflict difficult from an early age, as it brings back memories of my parents arguing with each other. It gives me a knot deep in my stomach, as if someone has kicked me.

I adjusted surprisingly well to working from home. I enjoyed being able to get out of bed later than my usual 6.30 a.m. I missed meeting colleagues for coffee, though, and soon started a bubble with my friend Ali. We would go for short walks during the week and meet every Saturday for a curry takeaway and a film. This has continued ever since March 2020, and has been a lifeline for me, in what has otherwise been an incredibly challenging period. The international travel restrictions greatly affected me. My long-awaited holiday to the Maldives was cancelled, although I continued to swim when possible. 'The chlorine kills the virus', joked the owner of the health centre I frequented.

One Saturday in March following the lockdown announcement declaring that everything was closed, including the swimming pools, I sat down in Victoria Gardens in Leamington and thought, *What now?* I had ten days of annual leave coming up which I did not wish to cancel. Then, as if by magic, I remembered 'wild swimming'. A friend had bought me a book on this subject for Christmas in 2018. Now was the perfect opportunity. I felt excited and visited the remaining shops that were open in search of a wetsuit, only to find children's wetsuits and nothing else. *Of course*, I thought to myself. *Who would expect to find an adult swimming outside in the UK at this time of year and during COVID?*

When I got home, I went online and found a wetsuit on Amazon. It even had purple, my favourite colour, around the seams. 'Neptune' arrived just in time for my leave, and I was relieved to find she was a perfect fit. Unfortunately, the boots and gloves would not arrive until May. Then I remembered that I had 'tuna' wet shoes. *They will do*, I thought. I got out my wild swimming book and in early April 2020, I set out to the Old Bathing Place near Stratford for my first wild swim.

Great, no swans, I thought, remembering my brother getting bitten by one when he was a young boy. I changed into my wet suit and sat with my legs in the water. It was freezing. A man started chatting to me, telling me I was brave, but the water froze my hands to ice. He started telling me how he had worked in Uganda, and then exclaimed, 'I've got some COVID-19 gloves in my car!' And off he went to get them. I reflected happily on the kindness of strangers at this time, and after putting on the gloves, I plunged into the icy water. I felt my heart beating with the cold, but soon felt refreshed and exhilarated, swimming round the water with the ducks. Getting out was a challenge, but afterwards I lay in the sun, content, relaxed, and feeling incredibly pleased with myself.

Old Bathing Place, Stratford

Wild swimming at Saxon Mill

I decided to go to Saxon Mill for my next swim. Ali and I did a long six-mile walk, and by the end, I was feeling very warm and excited to get in the water. This was to the amazement of a French family, whose children watched me from the bridge. The current of the water was extraordinarily strong, and as I swam, I hardly seemed to move. Yet the fast flow of the water made it warm and very exhilarating. It was helpful to have Ali to unzip me, although I was secretly pleased that I had mastered the art of doing it myself.

On Thursday, 9 April, I set off to Marcliffe after I had luckily found my wetsuit boots and gloves at my door. I arrived and parked nervously, as there were signs saying, 'No Parking'. I felt very naughty ignoring them all, and carefully searched the river for my entry point. It was a beautiful sunny day, and I could feel that my confidence had grown. I slithered into the water, which felt much warmer with my extra equipment. I swam peacefully up the river, enjoying the waves gently lapping beside me. My worries of getting out soon abated as there was a wooden jetty that I could use to pull myself up. I put all my gear on the wooden platform and lay on the grassy banks of the River Avon, feeling very content. Passers-by stopped to ask me about my experience and seemed extremely impressed. One commented, 'I have been to the Maldives … you'd love it there'.

Swimming in the River Avon, Marcliffe

On Easter Friday, I returned to the Old Bathing Place in Stratford, feeling more confident, especially with my gloves and boots. I found myself thinking of novel places I could try next, including a shallow river near Offchurch, although I was a bit worried that I might be like a flat fish scraping along the bottom.

On Easter Sunday, I set off for my fifth swim. I could not wait to get in the water from the jetty, which felt very warm after an initial cold shudder. A couple chatted to me, and the man said, 'Look out for the pike, they might be hungry'. I joked back, saying, 'I cannot feel them nibbling my toes', whilst his partner kindly took a photo for me. This made me think, 'I wonder what is inside this river?' I soon shrugged the thought off. I thought to myself, *Well, I may be locked down, but I have still found a way to be wild.* It was certainly a brilliant way of dealing with COVID. However, I did soon discover that the government was allowing water companies to pollute the waterways with sewage, so for anyone taking up this activity, I recommend sticking to clean water.

COVID restrictions lifted a little in August 2021. However, WOMAD (World of Music Arts and Dance) Festival, which I usually go to, was cancelled. Determined to get away to the sun, I decided to go to a COVID-free island, Kynthos, in August. I went on a group walking holiday and took a further week's leave to do my own thing. There were three of us on the trip, one of whom had been before and knew the guide.

It was a brilliant week, spent walking on the beautiful island and snorkelling as well. I got on well with the guide and his friend Mathias. The following week, after the others had travelled to another island, I hired a car and drove around the rest of the sites on the island, and we met up at beaches and went snorkelling. With Mathias' encouragement, I snorkelled far out to another island and saw brilliant sunsets. It was a great trip. I walked up to the cathedral and met a German woman who we later went for dinner with, and the next day we travelled together to the castle. Unfortunately, we were running late when we reached our accommodation. I desperately stopped to have a much-needed drink, then started driving to drop her off before realising I had lost my mobile,

I quickly rushed back and saw it in the middle of the road, outside the café. I happily picked it up, then realised that something must have run over it as the whole screen was damaged. This was not good news as all the details for my flights and accommodation were on the telephone. I went to see if Mathias could assist me, but I could not access my emails without my telephone, so I was stuck. He suggested I go back to the mainland a day earlier and buy a Greek phone, and reluctantly I decided that this was the best idea. I had loved being on Kynthos and found it very relaxing, so I was sad to leave a day early. I stayed in a hotel close to the airport. In the end I had to buy a Greek mobile phone. I flew back to the UK the next day and telephoned my insurance company, who instantly sent out a replacement.

Later in the year, I spoke to Clarissa regarding a need to review the CLAMP project we had set up for urban refugees in Uganda. I was enthusiastic about getting away from the lockdown in the United Kingdom over the festive season. My colleague and Ugandan organiser of the CLAMP project sent me a letter so I could travel, and I flew out to Uganda just before Christmas. I was incredibly happy to be in the sun, and the day after I arrived, the hotel manager announced that swimming pools could now open.

I also linked up with Emmanuel, my driver, and visited Lake Mburu National Park for three nights. It was wonderful to see all the animals and stay in a lovely tent with an eco-shower and proper bed. It was so relaxing hearing the birds and insects at night. One day, we cycled just by the boundary of the park, where you could get close to the animals. We visited a beautiful hotel and swam in their pool, enjoying the magnificent views.

When I returned to the UK in January 2021, I had to isolate for ten days. The UK was in lockdown, and I was working full-time from my house. I felt fed up but tried my best to take a day at a time, continued writing, and saw Ali, my bubble friend. I also decided to find a painter to paint the upstairs of my house. I fitted curtain rails, removed my already dilapidated shed, cleared out my rooms, and had a South African flag painted in bright colours on the side of my house. My garden looks very cheery now. It was too cold to start wild swimming in rivers in April, unlike last year, but I found a heated outdoor swimming pool in Banbury and have been swimming there, with my wetsuit on to keep out the cold.

Back in the UK, and despite the continuing challenges of COVID, I have submitted several research grants with colleagues in Africa to try to achieve my goal of building more contacts that could lead to future opportunities. Unfortunately, I think due to COVID, BREXIT, and a global recession, research grants seem much harder to get.

However, I did manage to secure $10,000 a year for the CLAMP refugee project through Clarissa's mental health clinics in America. I also made the difficult decision to retire from the health service and cut down to part-time working so that I could focus on other creative activities.

I finally retired at the end of April 2022. Although it felt strange and like a loss in many ways, it has freed up the time that I desperately wanted to focus on my writing and pursuit of opportunities in Africa.

In May 2021, I took a few days off and booked an Airbnb in Mumbles. I love the Gower coast and often stayed there during summers when I was at university. I have stayed connected with my friend Ros, who lives in Mumbles. It was a brilliant week; I stayed in a cosy cabin five minutes' walk from Mumbles centre and ten minutes' walk from Ros. When I arrived, I went for a lovely walk from Rotherslade Bay to Brandy Cove, which I had never been to, past Langland and Caswell Bay. The following day was windy and rainy with spurts of sunshine, so I took myself off to Penmaen and walked to Tor Bay and then to Oxwich. It was very blustery and exhilarating, and at several points I thought I might be blown off the hillside. I returned to Mumbles and walked into the centre to an outdoor café to meet my friend Richard. It was pouring with rain by then, so we had a cup of tea under the shelter and then went to get an Indian takeaway, which we took back to my Airbnb, and ate while watching a film. It was good to see him after a year of only speaking on the telephone.

I also took my Ghanaian *gyile* (wooden xylophone) with me so that I could continue my online lessons with Ben Lawrence on Tuesday and Thursday mornings. I enjoyed waking up to playing music in the mornings. The next day, I went to Port Eynon and walked along the beach, then drove to Mewslade. I walked from there out to Rhossili Bay and Worms Head, which was a beautiful walk. Around the coast from Mewslade was very hairy and high, and at one point I was only on what looked like a track for goats with a vertical cliff below me. It was very scary, and I was relieved to be back on solid ground after I had walked around. Ros invited me for a lovely dinner, and it was brilliant to catch up face-to-face after so long over a bottle of sparkling wine. She told me that she had a big birthday coming up, which I could not believe, and was so pleased I had taken the time to visit her. The thought of possibly never seeing her again was awful. I reflected afterwards on how we get caught up in our own lives and before we know it, friends and relatives have died. My parents dying within a year had brought this home to me.

The following day, I decided to walk from Rhossili along the beach to the island at the end and back, which ended up being over ten miles long. I could hardly believe I had walked so far. Then I went back down onto the beach to take photos of Helvetica, the wreck of a trawler, which had been in the sand since running aground in the 1980s. That evening, I packed my bags with a heavy heart, and the following day I managed to swim in a wetsuit at Rotherslade Bay and then walk to Caswell Bay before driving home. I had a lovely day but was sad to leave.

In July 2021, I was unable to travel as planned to Portugal due to restrictions. As luck would have it, I found a trip to the Orkney Islands for five days. I was excited to fly to Inverness and stayed a night and enjoyed a walk by the river. I then met the group at the train station, and we travelled to Orkney by train, boat, and bus. I particularly enjoyed the boat and passing the Man of Hoy, a large rock formation in the sea. The holiday was interesting, and we walked up to the highest point on the island to see all round the coast and the other islands. We also enjoyed meals out and a tour of the town, as well as whisky tasting. On a sunny day, I found a beach with a wreck of a boat on it and went snorkelling. When my lips started freezing, I got out. A friendly woman with her dog came along and chatted to me. I could not get over how big the dog was and took a photo of it in front of the wreck. It looked bigger than the boat at that angle. The group were friendly, and we all got on very well. Sooner than expected the trip ended and we were heading back to Inverness and then home.

In 2021, I planned with my friend Ali to have a joint sixtieth birthday party in November for both of our birthdays. This was an extremely exciting and fun event. We chose the Irish Centre in Leamington Spa as our venue, as we had loved it when we previously shared our fiftieth birthdays there. We had three performances from Ben's Ghanaian xylophone music, Seby's Ugandan group, as well as the Sambassadors of Groove Samba band. It was fantastic to have all our friends together listening and dancing to the music. I was immensely proud to perform in all the groups playing timba drum in the Samba band, *gyile* (Ghanaian xylophone) in Ben's group, and *endongo* (Ugandan thumb piano) in Seby's group. The atmosphere at the party was electric and fun. A few of us who were reaching sixty years of age soon performed a hilarious wild swimming sketch to 'bobbing along' music from the film *Bed Knobs and Broomsticks*, which went down very well.

The Sassy Splashy Synchronised Swimmers

Left to right: Anna, Ben, and Me performing *gyile*
(Ghanaian Balafon)

Left to right: Vieux, me (playing the *endongo*), Seby, Lucas and Ben

Sambassadors of Groove performing at the Irish Centre

In terms of travelling, things became more relaxed, and I managed to join a walking trip in Madeira. I also made it to South Africa in December and January 2022. This was a dream come true, and we visited Kruger National Park and the Drakensberg Mountains. I loved the mountains and went horse riding amongst the stunning scenery of towering mountains, lush green forests, and beautiful flowers. I also visited São Tomé and Príncipe, two islands in the Gulf of Guinea, where the three of us on the tour were the only tourists. I am also doing a tour of West Africa soon, visiting Guinea, Liberia, and Sierra Leone, which I am looking forward to.

It was a big decision for me to retire from the NHS, as I have worked there for over thirty years, but the timing felt right to pursue my own personal dreams. I was hoping the two research grants I submitted with the University of Cape Town to work in Cape Town, Durban, and Johannesburg would be successful, but unfortunately, they were not. I am still determined to live and work in Africa one way or another.

Writing this autobiography has helped me to reflect on my life and how far I have come, despite all the obstacles I have faced. I still look forward to a future in Africa as I move towards retirement and further adventures. As a Ugandan proverb says, '*Akwate Mpola Atuuka Wala*', which translates as: 'If you walk slowly, you will reach far'.

This, to me, has always been good advice, which I will take forward into the future.

References

Blom-Cooper Sir L., Brown M., Dolan R. & Murphy E. (1992) *Report of the Committee of Inquiry into Complaints about Ashworth Hospital*, Cmnd 2028, Vol. 1 and 2, (Chairman: Sir Louis Blom-Cooper), London: HMSO.

Chipchase, H. & Liebling, H. (1996) *Case File Information from Women Patients at Ashworth Hospital: An Explanatory Study*, Division of Criminological & Legal Psychology, Vol. 25, pp. 17–23.

Committee of Inquiry into Complaints about Ashworth Hospital (Blom-Cooper Inquiry) (1999; 2002), Vol. 1 and 2.

Cooke, D. J. (1991) *Psychological Impact of Prison Riots on Prison Staff in Scotland* (Simon Boddis, Ed.,). Her Majesty's Prison Service Psychology Conference Proceedings, held at the Hotel St. Nicholas, Scarborough, October 16–18, pp. 133–43, Office of Justice Programs.

Daily Record (2012) 'Bar-L Unlocked: In 1987 Prisoners Blamed Brutality behind Bars for Riot', *dailyrecord.co.uk,* last updated 24 July 2011, https://www.dailyrecord.co.uk/news/scottish-news/bar-l-unlocked-in-1987-prisoners-blamed-1108744.

Isis-WICCE (1999) *The Short-term Intervention of the Psychological and Gynaecological Consequences of Armed Conflict in Luweero District; Uganda*, Report, Isis-WICCE, Kampala, Uganda, www.wipc.org.

Liebling, H., Kinyanda, E. & Clamp, P. (2022) *CLAMP: Bringing Mental Health and Psychosocial Support to Urban Refugees,* The Global Compact on Refugees UNHCR, last updated 28 April 2022, www.globalcompactrefugees.org.

Liebling, H. (2018) 'Personal Reflections on working with Survivors of Sexual and Gender-based Violence & Torture', In, *In/visible Traumas: Healing, Loving, Writing*, Pujolràs-Noguer & Hand (Eds.).

Liebling, H. (2012) 'Experiences of a Young Girl Abducted by the Lord's Resistance Army, Northern Uganda', *Psychology of Women Section Review,* Vol. 14, Issue. 1, Spring, pp. 44–48, British Psychological Society, Leicester.

Liebling-Kalifani, H., Mwaka, V., Ojiambo-Ochieng, R., Were-Oguttu, J., Kinyanda, E., Kwekwe, D., Howard, L. & Danuwell, C. (2011) 'Women War Survivors of the 1989–2003 Conflict in Liberia: The Impact of Sexual and Gender-Based Violence', *Journal of International Women's Studies*, Vol. 12, Issue. 1, pp. 1–21.

Liebling. H. & Baker, B. (2010) 'Justice and Health Provision for Survivors of Sexual Violence in Kitgum, Northern Uganda', *African Journal of Traumatic Stress,* Vol. 1, Issue. 1, pp. 22–31.

Liebling. H. & Baker, B. (2010) *Justice and Health Provision for Survivors of Sexual Violence: A Case Study of Kitgum, Northern Uganda,* LAP Lambert, Germany.

Liebling-Kalifani, H. (2009) *A Gendered Analysis of the Experiences of Ugandan Women War Survivors,* VDM Verlag.

Liebling, H., Marshall, A., Ojiambo-Ochieng, R., Kakembo, N., Bendelow, G. & Liddle, J. (2007) 'Experiences of Women War-Torture Survivors in Uganda: Implications for Health and Human Rights', *Journal of International Women's Studies,* Vol. 8, pp. 1–17.

Liebling, H. (2004) 'Phil Strong Memorial Prize: Women war survivors in Luwero District, Uganda', *Medical Sociology News,* Vol. 30, Issue. 1, pp. 36–41.

Liebling, H. & Chipchase, H. (2000) Positive Approaches to Women who Self-Harm. In Positive Directions for Women in Secure Environments, R. Horn & S. Warner (Eds.) *Issues in Forensic Psychology 2.* The British Psychological Society for the Division of Forensic Psychology, pp. 22–26.

Liebling, H., Lovelock, C., Chipchase, H. & Herbert, Y. (1998) 'Working with Women in Special Hospitals, (J. Williams, Ed.). 'The Spoken Word', *Journal of Feminism & Psychology,* Vol. 8, Issue. 3, pp. 357–69.

Liebling, H., Chipchase, H. & Velangi, R. (1997) 'Why do Women Harm Themselves? Surviving Special Hospitals', *Feminism & Psychology,* Vol. 7, Issue. 3, pp. 427–37.

Liebling, H. & Chipchase, H. (1995) Women who Self-Harm, *Counselling News,* p. 20.

Liebling, H. & Chipchase, H. (1993) 'A Pilot Study on the Problem of Self-Injurious Behaviour in Women at Ashworth Hospital'. *Division of Criminological & Legal Psychology,* Vol. 35, pp. 19–23.

Musisi, S., Kinyanda, E., Liebling, H., Kiziri-Mayengo, R. & Matovu, P. (1999) *The Short-Term Intervention of the Psychological and Gynaecological Consequences of Armed Conflict in Luwero District Uganda,* Isis-WICCE Research; & Medica Mondiale, Isis-WICCE, Kampala, Uganda.

Report of the Committee of Inquiry into the Personality Disorder Unit, Ashworth Special Hospital (1999) Volume 1, Presented to Parliament by the Secretary of State for Health by Command of Her Majesty, January 1999, Cm 4194-i.